Reclaiming Public Education by Reclaiming Our Democracy

David Mathews

D1498983

KETTERING FOUNDATION PRESS
Dayton, Ohio

For information about permission to reproduce selections from this book, write to:

    Permissions
    Kettering Foundation Press
    200 Commons Road
    Dayton, Ohio 45459

This book is printed on acid-free paper
First edition, 2006
Manufactured in the United States of America

ISBN-13: 978-0-923993-16-0
ISBN-10: 0-923993-16-9
Library of Congress Control Number: 2005938130

CONTENTS

ACKNOWLEDGMENTS

In an earlier book, *Is There a Public for Public Schools?*, I thanked former Governor of Mississippi William F. Winter, a Kettering Foundation trustee, who gave the foundation an insider's perspective on the school reforms of the early 1980s. And I thanked the late Lawrence Cremin, another trustee and prize-winning American historian, who suggested that the foundation investigate what was happening to the social and political mandates that had driven the nineteenth-century commitment to public education. I remain grateful to them and also to Mary Hatwood Futrell, who chairs Kettering's board. She tested drafts of this new book in her graduate courses at George Washington University and was a wellspring of good advice. (Harris Sokoloff also tested the manuscript at the University of Pennsylvania.) I am indebted to all the trustees and to my colleagues at Kettering who helped organize the research for this volume. Connie Crockett, Randall Nielsen, Maxine Thomas, and Carolyn Farrow-Garland, in particular, ably directed most of the studies done for Kettering.

Research by The Harwood Institute, Doble Research Associates, and Public Agenda has continued to hold up well over the years, and I drew heavily on their recent findings—always with admiration for their good work. The footnotes and bibliography identify other helpful sources.

Ken Barr and Rebecca Rose were the latest in a large company of researchers who investigated countless sources and checked all of the details I overlooked. Juliet Potter, a model of thoroughness, took responsibility for the quantitative data. No one went over the manuscript more often than Anne Thomason, and her attentiveness saved me from innumerable errors. Harris Dienstfrey, who has excellent instincts about organization, followed Judy Suratt, a superb editor. They did the initial reviews. Most recently, Paloma Dallas helped me be clearer about the ideas introduced in the text.

I was delighted when Kathy Heil rejoined the foundation and took up the preparation of the manuscript. Angel George Cross, a wizard at the computer, had been doing that, capably assisted by Katie Runella. I value their patience and skill. Finally, our senior editor, Melinda Gilmore, checked the footnotes and the editing. Ever diligent, she has been our chief organizer. Among her duties were finding copy editors, Patricia Henrich and Linda Robinson. Melinda also selected a graphic designer, Steve Long, and an indexer, Lisa Boone-Berry.

I especially appreciate the citizens and civic organizations that provided examples of ideas in action. And once again, my thanks to the people who traveled to the foundation to share their research and criticisms. They helped me see the difference between what I said and what I intended to say.

Margaret Dixon, my assistant for more than 20 years, deserves special recognition for keeping our office in its proper orbit. And Mary Mathews, who was revising a book of her own while I was finishing this one, was more than a silent partner. She has always kept my entire world in its orbit while I write.

INTRODUCING A REVISION

The adults who have the most direct influence on young people include their parents, relatives, teachers, principals, coaches, and next-door neighbors. But these aren't necessarily the people who make the decisions about school policies. Ironically, those with the greatest opportunities to shape the lives of the next generation "are at the end of a long chain of authority stretching from 1600 Pennsylvania Avenue through state capitals to districts to local schools and finally into classrooms."[1] This book was written for people who may see themselves at the bottom of that pile. I believe there are ways for them to enrich our schools and, at the same time, reinvigorate our democracy, which is inseparable from education.

People's sense that they can't influence what happens in the public schools is a symptom of a deeper problem. In 1996, the Kettering Foundation published *Is There a Public for Public Schools?* (which I'll call *Is There?* from now on). It reported on a decade of studies that all pointed to one alarming conclusion: many Americans doubted the public schools were really their schools. They weren't just critical of the instruction; they didn't think there was much they could do about any of their concerns. They couldn't change the schools, and the schools appeared to be incapable of reforming themselves.[2] People's inability to make a difference was confirmation of their lack of

---

[1] In a chapter entitled "A Solution That Lost Its Problem: Centralized Policymaking and Classroom Gains," Larry Cuban argued that the people who are viewed as the problem in education (members of local boards and their agents) are the very people who are in the best position to solve the problem because of their direct influence on children. His chapter appeared in *Who's in Charge Here? The Tangled Web of School Governance and Policy*, ed. Noel Epstein (Washington, DC: Brookings Institution Press, 2004), p. 104.

[2] Paul Hill found high schools still resistant to change in his 2001 article, "Breaking the Hermetic Seal," *School Administrator Web Edition* (March 2001). After *Is There?* was published, studies done by the Annenberg Institute continued to find that "in some places, support for public education has worn perilously thin." Annenberg Institute on Public Engagement for Public Education, *Reasons for Hope, Voices for Change* (Providence, RI: Annenberg Institute for School Reform, 1998), pp. 13-14.

ownership.[3] Citizens reasoned that if they really owned the schools, they could help make the improvements in them they would like to see; otherwise, they couldn't be held responsible for what the schools did. This perception is not just a school problem; it is a serious political problem.[4]

Reclaiming Public Education by Reclaiming Our Democracy picks up on the loss of public ownership and discusses what might be done about it. The first thing that can be done to reconnect the public and the schools is to recognize that there are significant differences between the way professional educators and most school board members see problems, make decisions, and go about their work, on the one hand, and the way citizens-as-citizens view problems, make decisions, and go about their work, on the other. Neither way is inherently better; each is appropriate for its group. The difficulty is that educators and citizens often pass like ships in the night, sometimes even using the same terms for problems but not with the same meanings. "Higher standards," for instance, is a phrase that citizens and educators both use, although they don't necessarily mean the same thing by it. These misunderstandings are common in the best of circumstances, but unfortunately, circumstances aren't always the best; educators and citizens can be in serious disagreement.[5]

In June 2005, research by the Educational Testing Service showed how wide the gap had become between educators and the citizenry—

---

[3] Few people, if any, actually say, "we want to regain ownership of our schools." But Americans do say, "we need to get our schools back" or "we want our schools back." Those remarks are usually made when some external authority has replaced local authority—for example, when the state government has taken control of a school district that has been financially irresponsible. So "ownership" is a word that interprets what people are saying; it isn't necessarily their word.

[4] For more on the erosion of institutions of local self-government, see Martha Derthick, *Keeping the Compound Republic: Essays on American Federalism* (Washington, DC: Brookings Institution Press, 2001).

[5] In the book, I have tried to distinguish teachers from administrators, but sometimes I lump them together as "educators." I don't mean to abandon the distinction, however. Teachers have told me that they have unique opportunities to engage citizens because they often have the closest association with them, particularly parents. Much remains to be written about how these ties could be used in public building.

specifically between teachers and parents.[6] As David Broder wrote after seeing the research, "Clearly the educators and the public are on different wavelengths when it comes to conditions in our schools. That is a real barrier to progress."[7] What these differences in perceptions and priorities are, why they arise, and how they might be overcome are questions I'll try to speak to.

———— ÷ ————

People's sense that they don't own the schools is also a major problem for American democracy. The perception in and of itself would be troubling enough, but it doesn't stand alone. Americans feel the same way about many other institutions they created to serve them, including the electoral system and the government. Citizens say they have been pushed out of politics by a professional political class. "The government is supposed to work for us," they complain, "we are supposed to be in charge." When political leaders have tried to respond to this criticism by offering better services for citizens, people have been quick to say, "we aren't customers, we *own* the store!"[8] This feeling of being dispossessed also influences the political climate in which schools operate.

Since this is a book about public education and democracy, it is necessarily about the interrelation of the two. While sermons on the importance of public schools in our democracy are common fare in our rhetoric, less is said about the importance of democracy to public education.[9] Does a democratic citizenry have any role in education

---

[6] For example, the Educational Testing Service found that a majority of Americans thought high schools needed major changes; most educators disagreed. Peter D. Hart and David Winston, *Ready for the Real World? Americans Speak on High School Reform: Executive Summary* (Princeton, NJ: Educational Testing Service, June 2005).

[7] David S. Broder, "Split over Schools . . . Parents and Teachers Disagree on Reforms," *Washington Post*, June 23, 2005.

[8] Americans' loss of confidence in government and the political system has been documented in a number of studies, and I reported on some of them in *Politics for People: Finding a Responsible Public Voice*, 2d ed. (Urbana: University of Illinois Press, 1999).

[9] See Susan Fuhrman and Marvin Lazerson, eds., *The Public Schools*, Institutions of American Democracy Series (Oxford: Oxford University Press, 2005). In particular, look at Clarence Stone's discussion of civic capacity and democracy in Chapter 9.

other than paying taxes to support schools? If it does, then schools have as much at stake in the well-being of democracy as democracy has in the well-being of public schools. More about this later, but for now I'll just say that I have more in mind than merely improving the interaction between individual citizens and the schools. More is at stake than pleasant relationships.

I believe that public schools need a citizenry that acts as a responsible public. *And that is what this book is really about—how a democratic public forms and works to improve the education of all Americans.* It's about democracy and, more specifically, the role of the public. Since there are many ways to define both "democracy" and "the public," I will be as clear as I can be about what I mean by both.

While not claiming to have the only correct definition of "democracy," I think it is self-government by a sovereign citizenry that exercises its power in communities, statehouses, and the nation's capital. How do citizens get such power? The short answer for me is that we get our power through our ability to join forces and act collectively both with other citizens and through institutions we create to act for us. It follows then, that in order for Americans to be sovereign (that is, to rule themselves), they must be able to direct the institutions they created to serve them. Those institutions include public schools. "Directing" in this context means to define the purpose or mission of institutions, not to control their day-to-day activities. Democracy is not micromanagement. However, if the citizenry can't determine the mission of institutions such as public schools, self-rule is seriously undermined.

The mission of public schools should grow out of the broad objectives of our democracy. And the first job of citizens is deciding on those objectives or purposes. Some political theorists may argue that the purposes of democracy are fixed—freedom, justice, and so on—and all that remains to be decided are the best means to those ends. I believe, however, that Americans must continually determine what the great principles of democracy mean in the context of changing times. And they have to chart a new course of action when those principles conflict—that is the essence of self-rule.

I equate democracy with self-rule for several reasons—though never to suggest that people can rule themselves without government. Self-rule is not the same as direct democracy. I like the term because self-rule is consistent with the literal meaning of democracy, which is "rule by the people." Our Constitution says that "We, the People" are the sovereign power in the country, a power I don't believe was delegated to the state once the government was created.[10] Self-rule characterized the distinctively American political system that developed on the frontier in the early nineteenth century, a system in which citizens joined forces to bring their collective strength to bear on common problems, and a system based on ideals of individual freedom, shared responsibility, and equity.

In a book aptly titled *Self-Rule*, Robert Wiebe tells the story of how citizen politics came to define democracy in frontier America—despite the ruling elite's preference for a republic and not a democracy.[11] Nineteenth-century self-rule grew out of barn raisings and town meetings; it was a sweaty, hands-on, problem-solving politics. The democracy of self-rule was rooted in collective decision making and acting—especially acting. Settlers on the frontier had to be producers, not just consumers. They had to join forces to build forts, roads, and libraries. They formed associations to combat alcoholism and care for the poor as well as to elect representatives. They also established the first public schools. Their efforts were examples of "public work," meaning work done *by* not just *for* the public.[12]

You can see public work going on in communities today in the simplest forms of collective action—maybe nothing more than people cleaning up their town to attract outside investors. Citizens take rakes and mowers to the local park. Municipal officials send in crews with dumpsters and heavy equipment to do what rakes and mowers can't.[13] Public work on a larger scale protects the environment, builds housing

---

[10] The controversy over what the Constitution meant by popular sovereignty is discussed in George M. Dennison's *The Dorr War: Republicanism on Trial, 1831 1861* (Lexington: University of Kentucky Press, 1976).

[11] Robert H. Wiebe, *Self-Rule: A Cultural History of American Democracy* (Chicago: University of Chicago Press, 1995).

[12] I took the term "public work" from Harry C. Boyte and Nancy N. Kari, *Building America: The Democratic Promise of Public Work* (Philadelphia: Temple University Press, 1996).

[13] More on how citizens act collectively can be found in *For Communities to Work* (Dayton, OH: Kettering Foundation, 2002).

for the homeless, and organizes efforts to rescue victims of unexpected disasters. The ability of citizens to produce things from public work gives them the power to be sovereign.

A great deal of public work has been done for and through education. Americans have wanted to improve the institutions of education because they have seen education as the best means to improve society. The rationale has been that although laws are formative, education is transformative. We have called on the schools to lift people out of poverty and to teach youngsters to respect one another. We have based our faith in self-government on having an educated citizenry schooled in democratic values. From the early days of the Republic through the New Deal and the Great Society, this faith has spawned a vast array of school programs funded by billions of tax dollars. The question now is, if Americans lose confidence that they can call on the schools to serve public purposes, where will they turn to make the improvements in American society that they want?

One thing is certain: Whatever happens to public education will certainly affect America's ongoing experiment in self-rule. That is the reason the public schools are ultimately accountable to democracy, not just to parents or taxpayers.[14]

Having sketched out what I believe are some of the problems behind the problems in public education and democracy, let me say a bit about what you will find on these pages. I don't want to mislead anyone into thinking that *Reclaiming Public Education* is completely new; still-relevant sections of *Is There?*, with revisions, have been included. There are also additions, three in particular. First, new material from Kettering studies done after 1996 has been added, along with research from other sources. For example, there is a discussion of changes in school policy, such as the passage of the No Child Left Behind Act of 2001, usually referred to as NCLB. Since 2001, testing has increased

---

[14] For histories of the public schools' relationship to democracy, see Carl F. Kaestle, *Pillars of the Republic: Common Schools and American Society, 1780-1860* (New York: Hill and Wang, 1983); David Tyack and Elizabeth Hansot, *Managers of Virtue: Public School Leadership in America, 1820-1980* (New York: Basic Books, 1982); and David Tyack and Larry Cuban, *Tinkering toward Utopia: A Century of Public School Reform* (Cambridge, MA: Harvard University Press, 1995).

and more information than ever is available on students' scores, yet Americans still list education near the top of their concerns. While people believe in having high expectations for students and want some testing to measure how well youngsters are doing academically, many are becoming concerned about unintended but far-reaching consequences of new laws and regulations. That isn't to suggest that people don't recognize improvements that have resulted from recent legislation. One of NCLB's objectives for publishing test scores, for instance, has been met—we are more aware of just how poorly some children are faring. Some children are being left considerably behind. This issue, described by professionals in the 1970s as an "achievement gap," is front-page news again.

Second, writing this book gave me an opportunity to respond to questions raised by readers of *Is There?* The foundation also solicited reactions from people asked to review early drafts of *Reclaiming Public Education.* Both groups wanted to know, if there isn't a public for the public schools, could there be? In order to answer, I had to broaden my focus from "schools" to "education." Education is a collective enterprise that goes beyond schooling, and Americans are more confident in their ability to improve *education* than to change *schools.* Yet citizen-led initiatives in education might do a great deal to reinforce schools. And putting schools in the larger context of all the institutions that educate may be critical to their success. Surely we don't expect schools to flourish in a vacuum.

The third major difference between this book and *Is There?* is that *Reclaiming Public Education* is much more explicit about the public. You may have already noticed that the way I refer to the public isn't customary, and I'll explain why. The point here is that we must have the public we need before we can have the schools we want. Yet a community may not always have the public its schools need—or that the community needs. That's why it is important to understand as much as possible about how a public forms, which I've called "public building."

Public building is done through collective or public work, and the citizenry that does public work is the public. So the public I am writing about is both the agent *doing* the work and the entity *created by* the work. What I am suggesting is something like this: Imagine a group of people playing baseball. The work of playing baseball makes the group into something they weren't as individuals. The playing makes them a team; it creates the team. The individuals become a team only by playing together. This is the sense in which I mean that public work creates the public or that public building is done through public work.

What may appear to be convoluted semantics has a purpose. It allows us to see the public in a new light as a dynamic force that creates itself in the process of doing its work. We normally think of the public as a static body—a group of people. It is more; it is a citizenry-in-motion. The motion is the public. This insight can be as powerful as the insight of physicists who realized that what appeared to be solid objects were also moving atoms joined together.[15] The concept has particularly interesting implications for efforts to engage the public.

Let me bring this notion of the public back to the schools. The public I am writing about is more than a grassroots of support for schools or even a citizenry that actively endorses a reform proposal or approves school standards. It is a *citizenry that continually makes or produces things through public work*; that is, through collective decision making and acting. An example of such a public can be found on the American frontier, where people joined forces to build schools, found libraries, and open museums. I'll say more in a few pages about what kind of public work can be done in today's circumstances.

I'll conclude with a brief overview of each chapter and the audiences I am writing for. The chapters fall into three major parts. The first three chapters describe forces that once connected schools and the public as well as the forces that have since pushed them apart. For instance, some of the current divisiveness grows out of frustration with the bureaucratic system that has developed around the schools. Not all of the divisive forces, however, originate within the schools. Citizens have developed attitudes that make it difficult for a responsible public to form. I'm talking specifically about a consumeristic mind-set, which is evident in a weak sense of public ownership.[16]

---

[15] I am indebted to a physicist at the University of Dayton, Leno Pedrotti, for this analogy.

[16] Paul Werth Associates, *Final Report* (Dayton, OH: Report to the Kettering Foundation, May 5, 2003).

The first chapters also expand on the foundation's concept of "the public." Looking at the public as a dynamic force (that is, as a citizenry joined in collective action or work) has particular implications for projects to rally support for the schools. Rallying support is necessary in some communities. But if the public is more than a body to be roused and enlisted, we might consider another kind of engagement, an engagement that taps into the dynamics of public work.[17] The work of making collective decisions and acting on them generates the political equivalent of the electricity that lights a lamp. Engagement could mean plugging into that current, rather than trying to grab the bulb. The bulk of this book is about how citizens and educators might generate and tap into public work.

The most obvious implication of thinking of the public as a dynamic force is that if citizens aren't in motion, if public work isn't going on, then there is no public. That is the reason the public that the schools require doesn't necessarily exist—ready to be enlisted like a group of voters. It has to form around public work. And that is why public engagement has to proceed or go along with school improvement. Because of both reasons, I began calling the sort of engagement I am proposing "public-building" engagement. It is citizens engaging citizens rather than schools engaging people.

One clarification: Reviewers often found it unusual to see "the public" referred to in the singular when it is more common to hear references to various "publics." "The public" seems to imply a homogeneous body. I am not saying that. I am simply referring back to "the public" that is implied in the phrase, "We, the People." We, in all of our diversity, are part of that sovereign entity, which is made up of citizens-in-action.

The second part, beginning with Chapter 4, elaborates on what I just referred to as the things that only the public can do, particularly in education. I wanted to respond to implicit, if not explicit, questions from many reviewers: Why is a public necessary? What can public work accomplish in education?

Because of reservations about the citizenry, many educators are hesitant to involve the public. Some insist that their responsibilities begin and end with their students. Maybe their reservations are

---

[17] As I recall, Cole Campbell, among others at the foundation, thought it essential to distinguish between the public as a political force and as a political body.

understandable if professionals don't see anything people can contribute. Chapter 4 takes up this issue and makes the case that what citizens produce through their collective efforts can make it easier for teachers, administrators, and school board members to do their jobs. Citizens joined with citizens are able to accomplish what no school board, superintendent, principal, or cadre of teachers can do alone.

This collaboration between the public and the schools is not necessarily the same as the numerous business and civic partnerships that already exist. So much has been written about those partnerships that I haven't felt the need to say more.[18] At Kettering, we have looked for collaboration that involves educators joining forces with citizens doing public work. These joint ventures could strengthen the public at the same time as citizens are creating more community resources for education.

Chapters 5 and 6 go back to the idea that the public is a force and describe the activities or practices that create the force, or "electricity" if you like that analogy. These practices are used in carrying out the tasks of public work. Take the everyday act of giving a name to a problem. It is a critical practice. Naming or describing a problem has to capture people's experience and concerns before they will begin to work on solving it. Unless the name reflects people's reality, the problem isn't really their problem.

The third and final part deals with a practical issue. Even if intrigued by the idea that the public is a dynamic force drawing its energy from the practices used in public work, people sometimes have difficulty figuring out how to incorporate this concept into what they do every day. Chapters 7 and 8 speak to those people—citizens, members of school boards, and educators. This is not a how-to book. Yet the foundation's research has implications for the way both citizens and professionals in education might overcome the obstacles that separate the public from the schools.

Chapter 7, addressed primarily to community organizations and citizens, isn't for civic saints, influential leaders, or important

[18] I found reports like those by Don Davies at the Institute for Responsive Education particularly helpful in tracking the growth of community partnerships and initiatives to involve parents. Don Davies, "The 10th School Revisited: Are School/Family/Community Partnerships on the Reform Agenda Now?" *Phi Delta Kappan* 83 (January 2002): 388-392.

stakeholders. It is for busy, preoccupied folks from anywhere and everywhere in a community. It is about how they can make a difference. The public work that empowers citizens is done best under certain conditions. This chapter identifies those conditions and discusses what people can do when conditions are less than favorable.[19]

The chapter also describes the distinctive characteristics of communities where a public has taken shape and become a force in combating problems, especially problems that never seem to go away, those that "take a village to solve." Democracy in those communities has been anchored in local, civic action and not just in laws and institutions.

I hope this chapter will illustrate the close connection between self-rule and collective responsibility—the willingness of people to own their problems.[20] Communities that have been able to bring public work to bear on education haven't depended primarily on outside resources. They have recognized and drawn on local resources, and then, if necessary, reached out for assistance. This isn't pick-yourself-up-by-your-own-bootstraps politics; it is civic action moving from within and then going out, not the reverse. These communities have been inventive, not imitative. Small groups of people began where they were with whatever resources they had, which they used in self-directed work. Then they connected the dots, creating larger civic infrastructures that were joined like the tiny creatures that form giant coral reefs.

It stands to reason that communities where collective responsibility is strong, where there is a willingness to own problems and work on them, are communities where public education and public schools are likely to flourish. Surely educators have a stake in the kind of

---

[19] At the risk of repeating some sources and lines of argument well known to academics, I have included some professional literature references for people who aren't professional educators. For instance, Clarence Stone had a brief but useful comparison of types of community participation in educational reform in "Linking Civic Capacity and Human Capital Formation," in *Strategies for School Equity: Creating Productive Schools in a Just Society*, ed. Marilyn J. Gittell (New Haven: Yale University Press, 1998), pp. 163-176.

[20] See Harry Boyte's work in *The Backyard Revolution: Understanding the New Citizen Movement* (Philadelphia: Temple University Press, 1980) and *Everyday Politics: Reconnecting Citizens and Public Life* (Philadelphia: University of Pennsylvania Press, 2004) as well as Vaughn L. Grisham Jr.'s research on *Tupelo: The Evolution of a Community* (Dayton, OH: Kettering Foundation Press, 1999).

democracy that promotes this sort of community. As Robert Putnam has written, "revitalizing American community life may be a prerequisite for revitalizing American education."[21]

Chapter 8 takes on the attractive but questionable assumption that if the schools do a better job, public trust will be restored and the alienation will end. It is a natural assumption. Improving school performance, however, may be a necessary but not sufficient condition for bridging the divide between the public and the schools. To the extent that the alienation grows out of a lack of ownership, something will have to be done to restore ownership.

If public ownership has to be restored, what does that imply for educators? Do they have to learn still more skills and somehow find the time to use them? Kettering's research suggests not. Professionals need only find ways to do what they normally do in a fashion that makes it easier, not harder, for the public to do its job.

Chapter 8 is also about what professional educators and citizens might do together. The chapter describes the ways some educators have plugged into public practices in order to solve immediate problems—and, at the same time, increased the capacity of people to work as a public. It ends with a suggestion for how professionals in schools might escape some of the downdrafts of distrust they encounter by repositioning themselves and their schools in the larger public arena.

As I wrote this final section, I was thinking particularly about members of local school boards. They are in a strategic position to do something about the lack of public ownership. And they have an enormous stake in whether the public takes responsibility for the schools—and whether there is a public in their community. Unfortunately, boards today are at risk of being isolated from the citizenry that elects them. Not all Americans consider these boards their agents, and they don't find board meetings receptive forums for discussing their concerns.

School trustees, hemmed in by a multitude of government regulations and bombarded by litigation, have their own frustrations.

---

[21] Robert D. Putnam, "Community-Based Social Capital and Educational Performance," in *Making Good Citizens: Education and Civil Society*, ed. Diane Ravitch and Joseph P. Viteritti (New Haven: Yale University Press, 2001), p. 87.

They struggle to cope with externally imposed restrictions, which many believe undermine their ability to act in the best interest of their schools. Rather than having a coherent mandate from the public, they find themselves buffeted by a host of very particular or categorical requirements, all made in the name of "the public." Unable to meet the expectations of citizens because of these restrictions, they face an often-contentious crowd at their meetings.

Even more serious, the very legitimacy of boards has been questioned by critics who characterize them as "vestigial organs, like tonsils or appendixes." Some boards have been singled out as "havens for political junkies, launching pads for mayoral aspirants, [and] bastions of ideological discontent." Almost everyone grants that trustees are well-meaning citizens, but critics suggest that these good folks would do better to take up some other cause like visiting nursing homes. This disdain isn't merely the grumbling of a few malcontents. Mayors, encouraged by state legislatures, have taken control of school boards in some cities. Given the pressure from all sides, it is hard to imagine how school boards can do their jobs without a responsible public that does its job.[22]

Although I am not writing about simply improving the relationship between citizens and educators, the tensions between the two show up in so much of the research that it is impossible to move on to the issue of public ownership without recognizing the problem. Without taking one side or the other, or assessing the validity of the charges and countercharges, I'll put the connection between the public and the public schools in a historical context. Stepping back sometimes improves our outlook. And I'll report on the kind of relationship many Americans wish they had with the schools, both as individuals and as members of a community. The central question is whether Americans have reached a standoff with the public schools. Or is what citizens want in their relationship with educators not all that different from what teachers and administrators want in their relationship with the public?

---

[22] Jay Mathews, "Are School Boards Really Necessary?" *Washington Post*, April 10, 2001.

PART ONE:

A STANDOFF BETWEEN CITIZENS AND SCHOOLS?

WHOSE SCHOOLS ARE THESE?

WHY PUBLIC/WHAT PUBLIC?

THE RELATIONSHIP WE HAVE/ THE RELATIONSHIP WE WANT

CHAPTER ONE
WHOSE SCHOOLS
ARE THESE?

Why should Americans think that the public schools are *their* schools? Ideally, these schools are "ours" because they are agents of the people. Their standards and goals reflect community purposes. Unfortunately, a good many people today no longer believe that they own the public schools or that they have the responsibilities that ownership implies. This is not an issue of whether people are confident that these institutions are doing a good job, feel close to them, and would pay taxes for their support. Ownership is a more fundamental issue: When people drive by a schoolhouse, will they say "this is *our* school" or only "that's *the* school"? What they say will influence the future of public education in America. I am not suggesting that a time will come when the public schools will close their doors. Still, I wonder what kind of institutions these schools will become if they are not ours. And I wonder what will happen to communities if the schools aren't theirs.

The Question of Ownership

At first glance, the answer to the question of whether there is a public for the public schools may not appear to be worth raising. Most Americans believe it's essential to have schools that are open to everyone. And they send 50 million of their children to them every year.[1] Some would insist that these millions are the public for the schools. And they would add that many communities are blessed with good schools. Gallup polls suggest that the number of people who think their local schools are doing a good job has increased. I say

---

[1] U.S. Census Bureau, *School Enrollment—Social and Economic Characteristics of Students: October 2002*, http://www.census.gov/population/www/socdemo/school/cps2002.html (accessed April 20, 2005).

"suggest" because other research shows that this increase may be a "false positive"; the approval rate drops when challenged.[2]

On the other hand, many Americans remain convinced that the nation's school system (as distinct from their local schools) is in trouble. Only 24 percent nationally give the public schools grades of A and B.[3] They doubt that they can turn the situation around and fear that teachers and administrators can't either.[4] They point to what they see as educators' inability to maintain discipline and uphold academic standards. On reflection, however, Americans acknowledge that schools are overwhelmed by problems not of their making: child abuse, a breakdown in the norms of responsible behavior, poverty.[5]

If we thought the schools were our responsibility, this web of problems surely would motivate us to rally around the schools. But we aren't all rallying around the schools. Instead, a number of us have drifted away from the public schools, looking for alternatives. For example, in 2003, over a million children were taught at home; that is a significant increase over the 850,000 who were homeschooled 4 years earlier.[6] Even those who aren't drifting away don't necessarily feel responsible for the schools. People without children enrolled often argue that parents are solely responsible. As for parents, they tend to feel accountable for their own children, not for children generally. Lack of a sense of collective responsibility is another symptom of the lack of a sense of public ownership.

---

[2] Public Agenda found that high levels of satisfaction with local schools evaporated at the slightest challenge or when the questions people were asked became more precise. Jean Johnson et al., *Assignment Incomplete: The Unfinished Business of Education Reform* (New York: Public Agenda, 1995), p. 12.

[3] Lowell C. Rose and Alec M. Gallup, "The 37th Annual Phi Delta Kappa/Gallup Poll of the Public's Attitudes toward the Public Schools," *Phi Delta Kappan* 87 (September 2005): 45.

[4] Gallup Organization, *Attitudes toward the Public Schools Survey*, Phi Delta Kappa Survey (May 2003).

[5] Peter D. Hart and David Winston, *Ready for the Real World? Americans Speak on High School Reform: Executive Summary* (Princeton, NJ: Educational Testing Service, June 2005), p. 2.

[6] The most common reason for preferring homeschooling is "concern about the environment of other schools" (31 percent). U.S. Department of Education, National Center for Education Statistics, "1.1 Million Homeschooled Students in the United States in 2003," *Issue Brief* (July 2004).

These are some of the reasons I continue to worry that too many Americans doubt that the public schools are really *their* schools, even if they recognize, at least intellectually, that schools serve communities as well as individuals, and even if approval of school performance has increased in recent years.[7] I remember a man in Newark, New Jersey, who, when asked who "owned" the local school, said he wasn't sure which level of government had jurisdiction. He was quite certain, however, that the school didn't belong to his community; it was *not,* he said with conviction, "our school."[8] In his case, the lack of a sense of ownership appears to have been tinged with a sense of alienation. The foundation continues to hear echoes of this man's reaction in its current research.

Kettering's findings also resonate with recent studies of the relationship between the public and the public schools. For example, people don't believe they "own" the standards that schools use to document their accountability. And Americans don't think that current efforts at "engagement" as called for in the No Child Left Behind Act restore broad ownership of the schools. Some communities appear to have little sense of owning their schools, which people sometimes attribute to a diminished sense of community. In others, people are quick to say the schools belong to them. The contrast makes the absence of ownership more striking.[9]

The lack of close ties between the public and the schools is also evident in issues that are of deep concern to citizens but are discounted by professionals in education and proponents of reform. Jean Johnson at Public Agenda has noted a "continuing disinterest among most academics and reformers in problems of order, discipline, student motivation and civility in schools."[10] The historic agreement with

---

[7] Wendy Puriefoy, "All for All: Citizens Say They Want to Support the Public Schools," *American School Board Journal* (April 2000): 36.

[8] Reported by a member of a Teachers College, Columbia University, research team that conducted a study of education in Newark for the Kettering Foundation in 1985-1986.

[9] Doble Research Associates, *Who Is Accountable for Education?* (Dayton, OH: Report to the Kettering Foundation, 2003), p. 10; Bryan Goodwin and Sheila A. Arens, *No Community Left Behind? An Analysis of the Potential Impact of the No Child Left Behind Act of 2001 on School-Community Relationships* (Dayton, OH: McREL Report to the Kettering Foundation, May 2003), pp. 23-27, 37; and Paul Werth Associates, *Final Report* (Dayton, OH: Report to the Kettering Foundation, May 5, 2003).

[10] Jean Johnson, letter to the author, April 14, 2005.

citizens that the schools were to develop both mind and character seems to have been broken, a breach of contract that deepens people's perception that they can't determine the purposes of schools.

People who don't think they (or their communities) own the schools aren't necessarily indifferent to them. Schools are financed with taxes, and the quality of instruction affects property values. Americans care about both, even if they don't have children enrolled. Furthermore, although citizens may be alienated by what they consider unresponsive school bureaucracies, they may wish they *could* do something to improve the situation.

Wendy Puriefoy at the Public Education Network believes a majority of Americans are "genuinely willing to get personally involved to make schools better" because they say they will vote in school board elections and mentor students.[11] I believe that is exactly what people would like to do. Yet their pledges of support don't necessarily mean they have regained ownership of the schools and are no longer alienated by school systems. Americans who are alienated from the political system still vote. But their ballots should not be taken as evidence that political alienation isn't a problem.[12]

The point I am making here is that the lack of public ownership of the schools is related to but distinct from approval of their performance and general support. In attempting to make that distinction in speeches, I have tried all kinds of analogies. For example, when the hometown baseball team wins, people approve of its performance. They identify with the team, but don't think they own it; they single out the owner for criticism if the team begins to lose regularly. People also contribute to good causes like the March of Dimes. But they don't think they own the organizations. People who own houses, however, have a different relationship to them than to sports teams and charitable organizations. When the roof shingles blow off in a storm (as mine did recently), they know they are responsible for replacing them, and they either make the repairs themselves or hire someone to do the job (I hired somebody).

---

[11] Puriefoy, "All for All," p. 36. Also see Public Education Network, *All for All: Strengthening Community Involvement for All Students* (Washington, DC: Public Education Network, 2000).

[12] The lack of correlation between political alienation and voting was documented in a study done by the League of Woman Voters. League of Women Voters, "Alienation Not a Factor in Nonvoting," http://www.lwv.org/elibrary/pub/mellman.htm (accessed April 21, 2005).

Halfway out the Schoolhouse Door

Although most people would like to stand by the public schools, many aren't sure they can; they've moved at least halfway out the schoolhouse door.[13] Americans believe the country needs public schools yet are torn between a sense of duty to support these institutions, on the one hand, and a responsibility to do what is best for their children, on the other. Ambivalent, they agonize over the dilemma. Reluctantly, some have decided that public schools aren't best for their children—or anyone else's.

As noted, champions of public schooling take comfort in studies like Gallup that show that a large majority of parents like their local schools.[14] This finding leads to the claim that the people who criticize the public school system don't know what they are talking about because they don't have any way of judging the system as a whole. This interpretation, however, masks erosion going on under the foundations of public education. The broad mandate that once tied the schools to an array of social, economic, and political objectives seems to be losing its power to inspire broad commitment. Americans reason that if the schools can't help individual children, they certainly can't help the larger community.

The same erosion of confidence has affected other institutions. Even though people like their local representatives in Congress better than they do Congress in general, the declining confidence in our system of representative government is both real and dangerous. While I certainly hope that approval of the job the public schools are doing is on the way up, I don't think approval and a sense of ownership are the same. Public ownership implies public responsibility. Approval doesn't.[15]

---

[13] The Harwood Group, *Halfway out the Door: Citizens Talk about Their Mandate for Public Schools* (Dayton, OH: Report to the Kettering Foundation, 1995).

[14] Rose and Gallup, "The 37th Annual Phi Delta Kappa/Gallup Poll," p. 45.

[15] I am often asked by educators, does public ownership result in better student performance? The question itself is telling because it assumes that academic performance is the standard for measuring everything that happens in education. Some have in mind not just academic performance in general, but scholastic achievement as it is defined by standardized tests. Several studies suggest that the answer is "yes." But that answer keeps other questions from being addressed. A democratic citizenry might ask about ownership because they value it as an end in itself. That is, they might say the first test of any institution that operates in the public's name is whether it is under the direction of the public.

Even among those happy with the public school their children attend, allegiance may be only to that particular institution, rather than to the cause of public education at large. When parents in a study were asked whether they would prefer public schools or alternatives such as private schools, most—including many who had spoken positively about their local schools—said they would "take our children out of public schools if we could."[16] And one journalist wrote pessimistically, "If I had to choose, I think most children would be better off with no public schools at all than with the ones we have now."[17] A decade later, the same sentiments still appear under headlines like "Let's Get Rid of Public Schools."[18]

How Ownership Is Lost

My argument so far goes like this: Too many Americans doubt the public schools are theirs, but the schools can't become vibrant, democratic institutions until the public reclaims them as its own. The rest of this chapter will explore the meaning and character of public ownership, why professional educators may be wary of citizens, and why communities may not have a citizenry that can take responsible ownership of the schools.

First of all, the kind of ownership I am talking about isn't the possessive sort that might foster an adversarial relationship with professionals. Public ownership expresses itself in civic work done on behalf of education. "Owning" public education is like owning a home; owners are busy keeping up the lawn, making minor repairs, and calling in professionals for tasks they can't handle. Owners in education do the same by providing internships for students in their businesses, organizing tutorial assistance for youngsters having difficulty in academic subjects, or participating in a seemingly trivial project like making snow cones for school-community picnics.

The nature of the work isn't as important as the sense of ownership that motivates it is. My colleague Maxine Thomas and I learned the importance of this distinction by observing a number of meetings

[16] The Harwood Group, *Halfway out the Door*, p. 13.

[17] Linda Seebach, "Government Runs Schools No Better Than It Would Churches," *Dayton Daily News*, January 19, 1995.

[18] David Gelernter, "Let's Get Rid of Public Schools," *Virginian-Pilot*, May 22, 2005. This article was originally a special to the *Los Angeles Times*.

in which school projects were being discussed. In some, the *principal* asked for volunteers to help out with school activities like picnics. In others, *citizens* identified problems they felt obligated to solve because of the way they understood their responsibilities. Then they decided on projects and parceled out the work among themselves. Maxine and I realized that there was a qualitative difference between the two cases, and it didn't have to do with the nature of the projects. Those who made snow cones for picnics out of a sense of responsibility as community citizens were doing something more meaningful than just making the cones.

The contributions made by citizens who think they are responsible for the schools are put to their best use when educators are receptive to civic initiatives. Unfortunately, that doesn't always happen. One teacher showed her hostility to outside influences when she argued that "teaching is like brain surgery"; she didn't want the community in her operating room. When Americans reach out and their efforts are rebuffed, they usually throw up their hands and walk away.

Citizens complain that educators are preoccupied with their own agendas and inattentive to people's concerns. In one study, the participants said the "greatest obstacle" to a better working relationship with schools was "the attitude of educators, especially administrators."[19] This perception intensifies people's feeling that the public schools aren't really theirs. And that makes them doubt the schools can ever be changed from the inside, even though that is what many citizens would prefer.[20] Schools are thought to be wedded to business as usual, a feeling so pervasive that bond issues are often rejected unless people have proof positive that specific improvements will definitely be made.[21]

Wary Professionals

Most teachers and administrators would deny that they want to keep community members out of the schools or that they are

---

[19] Doble Research Associates, *Public Schools: Are They Making the Grade?* NIF Report on the Issues (National Issues Forums Institute, 2000), p. 2.

[20] Rose and Gallup, "The 37th Annual Phi Delta Kappa/Gallup Poll," p. 46.

[21] Gerald Johnson, "The Wrong Track: Why Alabamians Believe the State and State's Public Education Are on the Wrong Track," *Alabama School Journal* 121 (June 7, 2004): 1 and Hart and Teeter, *Equity and Adequacy*, p. 1.

indifferent to people's concerns. They would insist that they spend considerable time listening to their fellow citizens. Even so, professional educators have difficulty conceiving of a responsible public because they have little or no experience with such a citizenry. And the experience they do have with citizens makes them wary.

It didn't take Kettering researchers long to realize that teachers are often frustrated by what happens in their relationship with the community at large. Teachers see the public arena as a world of social problems that fester outside the classrooms and eventually find their way inside. The effect of these problems can be devastating. As one teacher in Houston, Texas, explained, "I spend 60 percent of my time on discipline, 20 percent on filing, and, if I am lucky, I have 20 percent left for instruction."[22] School personnel say they have to shoulder more and more of the immense responsibility of raising children, even to the point of feeding and supervising them after school because parents aren't meeting their responsibilities.[23] No wonder teacher morale is low.

Other encounters with the citizenry are often equally unhappy. Teachers complain that they are captives of externally imposed reforms, with little or no voice.[24] And administrators, battered by interest groups, become guarded, convinced that "You can't just pull together a group of people from the community to tell educators what to do." The perception that the public has nothing to offer is apparently widespread. One veteran educator of 25 years confessed to

---

[22] Jim Mathews, conversation with author, 1995. Also see Public Agenda, *Teaching Interrupted: Do Discipline Policies in Today's Public Schools Foster the Common Good?* (New York: Public Agenda for Common Good, May 2004).

[23] Doble Research Associates, *Expectations and Realities: An Analysis of Existing Research* (Dayton, OH: Report to the Kettering Foundation, January 2004), p. 27.

[24] One of the teachers who reviewed a draft of this book was very clear about the frustrations of teachers and projects to "empower" them. Reforms were handed down from on high, this teacher said; typically, she and her colleagues were only "empowered" to implement what others had decreed. When a new grant program would introduce a new set of reforms, the pattern would be repeated, leaving teachers cynical about being "done to." The foundation has found the absence of a sense of agency widespread in other groups of educators, as well as members of school boards. See Connie Crockett, "Conversations with Preview Readers of *Public Building for Public Education*" (Dayton, OH: Kettering Foundation, June 2005).

me, "I was trained to counter influences from outside my classroom, not to work with the public."[25]

Scholars have pointed out that professional educators aren't prepared to involve citizens as citizens because it doesn't fit with the concept of democracy implicit in their training. It seems that people can get credentials in public education without ever having to consider what "public" means. And the skills they are taught, such as bargaining or negotiation, wouldn't be useful if they did encounter a citizenry acting as a collective public rather than as an aggregation of interest groups.[26]

I'll say more about the tensions between citizens and educators in Chapter 3, but there are bright spots in the relationship. For instance, professionals in education usually pay attention to mothers and fathers. In fact, they often equate parents with "the public." Listening to parents, however, is a necessary though not sufficient step toward engaging the public. Even if all the people with school-age children were supportive, it wouldn't provide the public that the schools need because Americans with school-age children are only about one-third of the population. That is not a large enough group to provide a true public mandate.[27]

The Absence of a Public

Maybe educators don't see a responsible public capable of taking collective ownership in education because, in fact, there isn't one. Communities vary in civic spirit and allegiance, and people's allegiances (along with their jobs and social ties) may be outside the school district. Demographics also change frequently; yesterday's city with strong institutional leaders and locally based industries might disappear. Even stable towns and neighborhoods may not have a working citizenry.

---

[25] In a discussion with reviewers of the first draft of this manuscript, it was suggested that teachers and administrators operate as the "street-level bureaucrats" described in Michael Lipsky's *Street-Level Bureaucracy: Dilemmas of the Individual in Public Services* (New York: Russell Sage Foundation, 1980). The autonomy education professionals do retain comes when the classroom doors close. Anything that keeps those doors open may threaten professional autonomy.

[26] Connie Crockett, "Readers of *Is There a Public for Public Schools?* A Report on Three Meetings" (Dayton, OH: Kettering Foundation, Fall 2001), p. 4 and Connie Crockett, "Notes from University Professors *Is There a Public?* November 29-30, 2001" (Dayton, OH: Kettering Foundation), pp. 1, 4.

[27] Jason Fields, *America's Families and Living Arrangements: 2003* (Washington, DC: U.S. Census Bureau, 2004), pp. 3-4.

Schools can't serve a community's purposes if citizens don't come together to make decisions about what those purposes are.

An obvious and prior issue is whether Americans are interested in being part of a citizenry that takes responsibility for its schools. A number of people, although uncertain about what steps to take, do indeed seem willing to become active citizens—*provided they can see the possibility of making a difference.* This willingness to become involved in community matters was documented in a study done for the League of Women Voters in 1999. A majority of those surveyed said they were involved, and 46 percent said they would like to be more active, while only 4 percent confessed that they wanted to be less active. Most made having a constructive influence on children their highest priority.[28]

To find out more about whether there could be a larger public for the public schools, Kettering looked at what community groups have actually done to take ownership and at the decisions citizens have made to act on a range of issues that affect schools directly and indirectly. Some of the evidence the foundation has of what Americans would be willing to do comes from one of the National Issues Forums (NIF) where people considered a range of options for improving public schools.[29] Results from these forums showed that participants were willing to accept the responsibilities of ownership, which did not mean they wanted to control "the day-to-day operation of the schools."[30] They wanted a closer relationship with the schools, not just as individuals but as a community. Adding to this evidence, a 2004 survey found that 57 percent of those polled said their community had come together to work on problems in education.[31]

[28] League of Women Voters, "Working Together: Community Involvement in America," http://www.lwv.org/elibrary/pub/cp_survey/cp_4.html (accessed April 22, 2005).

[29] Although called National Issues Forums, most issues in this forum series are important to communities and require local action. The forums are convened by civic, educational, and religious organizations across the country. For more information, visit the National Issues Forums Institute Web site at http://www.nifi.org.

[30] Doble Research Associates, *How People Connect: The Public and the Public Schools* (Dayton, OH: Report to the Kettering Foundation, June 1998), pp. 2-3.

[31] Public Education Network and *Education Week, Learn. Vote. Act.: The Public's Responsibility for Public Education* (2004), p. 5. The Kettering Foundation records also showed that of nine communities that had participated in the community politics workshop, five had worked on issues in education.

Although the studies indicate a latent sense of civic responsibility and the potential for collective action, they don't justify the conclusion that there is a public continually at work in every community. I just cited the most positive poll, which showed that 57 percent of citizens said their community had come together to work on a problem in public education. But the pollsters admitted that the responses also indicated "limited personal participation," which had actually declined between 2001 and 2004. Participation was also individual rather than collective in most cases. People counted attending sporting and other school functions as being involved. Only about one in four had worked in a civic group that supported schools. Even though 53 percent said they would be willing to join such a group, the study did not delve into what would prompt them to act on this inclination.[32] Usually people added the caveat that they would get involved if they could make a real difference. But that is precisely what many say they can't do.

Other studies contend that people no longer have time for such collective projects because they are absorbed by their own private interests. And still other research has found that Americans believe that the very sense of community is being lost—though they regret it. Most recognize that they have civic obligations, even if they aren't sure that others share their sense of duty. In fact, some people are quite passionate about the need to make a difference in their community, particularly when the education of the next generation is at stake. As a man in Portland, Oregon, said to the people around him, "We sit here and we criticize public schools—they're awful, they're no good. But who the hell's going to change it?" Then he answered his own question: "We are. We're going to change it. In your life you've got to do something. Everybody's got to do something."[33]

Despite citizens' frustrations over not being able to act on their concerns, I believe they know, deep down, that they and their communities are ultimately accountable for the education of a new generation—along with teachers and administrators. Note again that I said "education" rather than "schools"; Americans make a sharp

[32] Public Education Network and *Education Week, Learn. Vote. Act.*, p. 14.

[33] The Harwood Group, *Halfway out the Door*, p. 19. This often-latent sense of civic duty was first reported in The Harwood Group, *Citizens and Politics: A View from Main Street* (Dayton, OH: Report to the Kettering Foundation, 1991). For a more recent study of attitudes toward public schools, see Doble Research Associates, *Expectations and Realities*.

distinction between the two. Education is learning outside the class-room as well as in; it's everyone's responsibility, everyone has a role to play in it, and so everyone is accountable.[34] In a meeting in Baton Rouge, a woman took this insight to its logical conclusion when she said there should be "a community strategy, not a school strategy, for educating every single child."[35]

The Case for Public Building

Readers of *Is There?* were struck by the thought that there might not be a public for the schools ready to be engaged. The possibility that the public has to be created suggests that enlisting individuals to support the schools isn't going to be enough. Certain things have to happen in communities before Americans will see the improvements they want in education—a public has to form. And that occurs as small groups of people join forces to work on common problems, including those in education. Their example can be persuasive—over time.

If there has to be a public in order for public education to flourish, why isn't public building on the agenda of every civic organization in the country? The man who said the schools didn't belong to his com-munity isn't the only person saying that. People's alienation from the schools is no secret. So, we shouldn't make the problem worse. If the supports for a bridge have deteriorated, sensible folk shouldn't keep driving eighteen-wheelers over it.

The encouraging news is that, although not necessarily focused on public building and ownership, a number of organizations have become concerned about the troubled relationship between the public and the schools. Their projects often fly under the banner of "public engagement." So many of these efforts have been launched that Robert Sexton, director of Kentucky's Prichard Committee, described public

---

[34] Doble Research Associates, *Summaries of Five Research Projects* (Dayton, OH: Report to the Kettering Foundation, 1995), pp. 1-5 and Doble Research Associates, *Take Charge Workshop Series: Description and Findings from the Field* (Dayton, OH: Report to the Kettering Foundation, 1993), p. 2.

[35] John Doble to Damon Higgins and Randa Slim, memorandum, "Report on CERI Community Leadership Workshop Baton Rouge, LA, 6/23/93," July 19, 1993, p. 4.

engagement as a "growth industry" when he surveyed the field.[36]
Less encouraging is news that many of these projects allow individual
citizens to be informed about and react to proposed reforms while
seldom envisioning a collective public acting on its responsibility as
owners of the schools.

Still, there are some engagement efforts that allow citizens to do
more than listen and react. These efforts may have been encouraged
by research showing that social capital is generated by public work.[37]
Social capital consists of networks that link people, norms of reciprocity, and trust. The capital generated by public work on one project can
be used to "fund" more collective enterprises.

Public Accountability?

Another compelling reason for public building is to stimulate public ownership of accountability. Public building increases the chances
that there will be what that woman in Baton Rouge wants: "a community strategy, not a school strategy, for educating every single child."
And a community strategy implies community accountability.

Today the emphasis is primarily on professional accountability
alone, which is one of the goals of the No Child Left Behind Act. It
was thought that publishing standardized test scores would make

---

[36] See Robert F. Sexton, "Introduction," in *Mobilizing Citizens for Better Schools*
(New York: Teachers College Press, 2004). He reviewed the main arguments for
public participation made by Anne Henderson, Richard Elmore, Paul Hill, Michael
Fullan, Susan Fuhrman, David Evans, and Linda Darling-Hammond, among others.

In a report to Kettering, Mid-continent Research for Education and Learning
described how public engagement is defined, using media reports, articles, and the
provisions of the No Child Left Behind Act of 2001. See Goodwin and Arens, *No
Community Left Behind?*

[37] At Kettering we've found it useful to identify those sources of social capital that
are political rather than just social. (Think of the difference between town meetings
and choral festivals.) We have used the term "public capital" to make that distinction. Public capital grows out of networks and norms of reciprocity, just as social
capital does, but is generated by public work. The literature we have drawn on for
social capital includes Robert D. Putnam, "Community-Based Social Capital and
Educational Performance," in *Making Good Citizens: Education and Civil Society*,
ed. Diane Ravitch and Joseph P. Viteritti (New Haven: Yale University Press,
2001), pp. 58-95 and Clarence N. Stone, "Linking Civic Capacity and Human
Capital Formation," in *Strategies for School Equity: Creating Productive Schools in
a Just Society*, ed. Marilyn J. Gittell (New Haven: Yale University Press, 1998), pp.
163-176.

educators more responsible by allowing parents to see and judge a school's performance.[38] Citizens, however, want more from the schools than academic achievement, important as that is. Picking up on what people are saying, a RAND study recommended that accountability be broadened to include "more of the public's goals for education."[39] That obviously requires a public that can set goals.

Although most people believe in high expectations for children and some testing, they don't consider testing alone a definitive measure of accountability.[40] Citizens want educators to be held responsible for what they do, but the word "accountability" appears to be more a legal and policy term than a concept important to people. Only 1 of 35 people involved in a recent study even mentioned accountability without prompting—and that was a school board member.[41]

If the public "owned" accountability—if citizens took greater responsibility for what happens in education—it could change the attitude Americans have toward schools. Public accountability is more relational than informational. That is, citizens are looking for more than the data from schools. They want a face-to-face exchange with educators and a full account of what is happening in classrooms and on playgrounds. They want to know what kind of people their youngsters are becoming as well as how they are doing academically. Americans have said that most legislated accountability measures don't do that; they still leave citizens feeling on the outside trying to look in.[42]

---

[38] U.S. Department of Education, *Questions and Answers on No Child Left Behind: Accountability*, http://www.ed.gov/nclb/accountability/index.html (accessed April 10, 2005).

[39] Brian Stecher and Sheila Nataraj Kirby, eds., *Organizational Improvement and Accountability: Lessons for Education from Other Sectors* (Santa Monica, CA: RAND Corporation for the William and Flora Hewlett Foundation, 2004), p. 124.

[40] Doble Research Associates, *Public Schools*, pp. 8-10 and Doble Research Associates, *Who Is Accountable for Education?*, pp. 1, 7-11.

[41] Doble Research Associates, *Reframing "Accountability": The Public's Terms* (Dayton, OH: Report to the Kettering Foundation, March 2001), p. 6.

[42] Goodwin and Arens, *No Community Left Behind?*, p. 37 and Crockett, "Readers of *Is There a Public for Public Schools?*," pp. 2-4.

If the public truly owned accountability, it would include all the owners. The accountability movement as it is now doesn't always include students or communities. Yet educating children involves so many people and forces, which no profession or group can control, that Americans are reluctant to hold any one party totally accountable. As said earlier, when Americans talk about the responsibility for education, they implicate a lot of people, not just teachers and administrators. They think of accountability as a "societal issue" rather than only a school issue.[43]

When citizens think about accountability, they are particularly concerned with the moral commitments of educators, not just their professional or technical competence. They look for dedication, caring, and high ethical standards. People are worried that conventional accountability may absolve professionals of what citizens consider educators' higher obligations.[44] For example, studies show that people value teachers who can encourage and inspire, who can make learning come alive, who are inventive in their classrooms, and who are patient in one-on-one relationships with students. Legal accountability standards, in contrast, emphasize teacher certification in subject matter and students' scores on tests.[45]

In sum, the case being made here is that full accountability can't be separated from public ownership and the public building work that generates ownership. Otherwise, accountability will serve only individuals who have children in schools. It will have less public meaning.

---

[43] Achieving high academic standards appears most likely when parents and teachers work as a team in a "'village' culture" of supporting agencies. These conditions have been found on military bases, where students do much better than their counterparts in other public schools. Anne T. Henderson and Karen L. Mapp, *A New Wave of Evidence: The Impact of School, Family, and Community Connections on School Achievement* (Austin, TX: Southwest Educational Development Laboratory, 2002), pp. 51-52.

[44] Mid-continent Research for Education and Learning, *Examining the Meaning of Accountability: Reframing the Construct, A Report on the Perceptions of Accountability* (Dayton, OH: Report to the Kettering Foundation, June 2004), pp. 3-5.

[45] Jean Johnson, "When Experts and the Public Talk Past Each Other," *Connections* (Winter 2005): 27.

High Stakes

Restoring public ownership of the schools through public building is both a democratic and an educational imperative. If the schools aren't seen as part of a collective effort to carry out a collective responsibility (education), doesn't that make them something like the public utility companies that provide us with water, electricity, and gas? These companies are essential to the economy and often contribute generously to schools, but they aren't public in the way schools are supposed to be. Public schools don't merely provide another service (instruction for our children), which we pay for with tax dollars rather than out-of-pocket fees. If that were all they did, we couldn't expect a relationship with them any different from the relationship we have with the companies that provide our utilities. Legislative bodies or commissions would set tax rates and supervise school services, but public ownership would be largely in name only —and community responsibility would be meaningless. If public schools become so removed from their communities that the schools are little more than "companies" financed with government revenue, then they will mean far less than they have meant historically.

What exactly have they meant? One way to answer that question is to look at the first schools that were called "public." Founded in the early nineteenth century, a time admittedly different from our own, the early public schools, nonetheless, were part of a still-relevant design for a democratic nation—and a still-valid strategy for establishing livable communities. Those schools had a relationship with the citizenry that has implications for schools today that struggle to engage their communities. The history of the creation of the first schools also sheds light on what the first public was like, not as an abstraction, but as a concrete, everyday citizenry-at-work. The next chapter elaborates.

CHAPTER TWO
WHY PUBLIC/
WHAT PUBLIC?

One of the people interviewed by Kettering researchers for *Is There?* questioned whether there had ever been a public for the public schools. Maybe some "deep thinkers" believed there had been such a public, she allowed, but no one else did. (I gather she was more than a little suspicious of "deep thinkers.")

Unable to ignore her doubts, I revisited the history of public education and then did my own investigation, examining the records of the first schools in southwestern Alabama, where I grew up. I wanted to find out who established them—and why. I thought this research would provide concrete examples of the public forming in communities and show what self-rule actually looked like. The results were published in *Why Public Schools? Whose Public Schools?*[1]

The way nineteenth-century Americans organized to provide schooling speaks to a troubling question readers ask today: What if there is no public where our school is located? What if people are invested solely in their personal lives, scarcely know their neighbors, and are too busy in their jobs to have time for the community? Those are real problems, but people living in frontier America also faced serious constraints on their time and energy in just surviving. Still, they managed to create a robust public life. How they did it is instructive.

Schools as a Means to Public Ends

According to national lore, the first schools called "public" were chartered to complete the "great work" of the American Revolution. They were as much a foundation for American democracy as the Constitution and the Bill of Rights. One historian, Rush Welter, observed

---

[1] Much of this chapter is adapted from *Why Public Schools? Whose Public Schools? What Early Communities Have to Tell Us* (Montgomery, AL: NewSouth Books, 2003).

that the new nation was able to allow individuals maximum freedom because schools, common to all, would see to it that social order prevailed. Americans opted for a system he described as "anarchy with a schoolmaster."[2] They relied on their schools to create one nation out of diverse populations that had brought legacies of bitter conflict from their homelands.

Social stability, however, wasn't our highest ambition. America was founded to write a new chapter in human history—to create a new civil order, an aspiration so fundamental that we stamped it on the one-dollar bill: *novus ordo seclorum.* Public schools were to be the agents of that aspiration. Americans reaffirmed that mandate in the Northwest Ordinance of 1787: "Religion, morality and knowledge, being necessary to good government and the happiness of mankind, schools and the means of education, shall be forever encouraged." Ever since, or perhaps until very recently, schools have been seen as the primary instruments for carrying out American objectives such as creating a more just society and defending the nation against the rival we once saw in the Soviet Union. Public purposes were as evident in the National Defense Education Act of 1958 as they were in the Northwest Ordinance.[3]

A broad mandate for public education emerged over time out of a wide-ranging debate; it eventually produced a synthesis that guided the country for the better part of two centuries. Public education was to

- create and perpetuate a nation dedicated to particular principles, especially individual freedom and social justice;
- develop a citizenry capable of self-government;
- ensure social order;
- equalize opportunity for all, thereby offsetting any class distinctions; and
- provide information and develop the skills essential to both individual economic enterprise and general prosperity.

---

[2] Rush Welter, *Popular Education and Democratic Thought in America* (New York: Columbia University Press, 1962), p. 4.

[3] For a full account of the role of political ideas in promoting public schools, see Carl F. Kaestle, *Pillars of the Republic: Common Schools and American Society, 1780-1860* (New York: Hill and Wang, 1983).

These objectives were thought to serve the interests of all, or the nation as a whole. To implement them, Americans not only built schools but also created libraries, museums, and a host of other educating institutions.[4] Most schools, though not all, were publicly controlled. Some were operated by religious organizations; others were proprietary institutions. Whatever their origins, all of these educating institutions were responsible for what Samuel Harrison Smith called the "general diffusion of knowledge." The rationale for this large investment in education was clear in the minds of American patriots like Smith, who wrote: "If happiness be made at all to depend on the improvement of the mind and the collision of mind with mind, the happiness of an individual will greatly depend upon the general diffusion of knowledge."[5]

Because public schools were one of the principal institutions serving the good of all, the public was obliged to support them. That was the corollary implied in the mandate from the citizenry. Public schools were agents for creating the kind of country Americans wanted, and so they merited everyone's allegiance. Such was the logic of the schools' contract with the public, the basis for a special relationship between the citizenry and the schools.

Public in Character and Operation

Initially, our schools were public in purpose, although not necessarily in character or operation; that is, they weren't free to all citizens. We have made our schools more fully public through a long struggle that has taken most of the nineteenth century and extended into the twenty-first. As a result of a nationwide common school movement during the early nineteenth century, public schools came to mean not only institutions paid for with tax funds and controlled by citizen boards but also schools common or open to all citizens. Admittedly, "all citizens" carried with it the nineteenth-century's definition of citizenship, which did not extend to women, most African

---

[4] Lawrence A. Cremin, *The Wonderful World of Ellwood Patterson Cubberly: An Essay on the Historiography of American Education* (New York: Bureau of Publications, Teachers College, Columbia University, 1965) and Lawrence A. Cremin, *American Education: The Colonial Experience, 1607-1783* (New York: Harper and Row, 1970).

[5] As quoted in Kaestle, *Pillars of the Republic*, p. 7.

Americans, or Native Americans. Still, the ideals behind the promotion of public schools, particularly justice and equity, were (and continue to be) a challenge to the prevailing restrictions.

What I have written up to this point summarizes what I wrote in *Why Public Schools? Whose Public Schools?*—with one major exception. Originally, I said that proprietary schools in the early nineteenth century served children whose parents could pay for them while the "free" or public schools supported with tax dollars were for the poor. That was an overgeneralization that needs to be corrected. Some free schools were for the poor, but our tradition isn't one of welfare-like schooling. Although different Americans had different reasons for supporting schools common to all, most agreed that public schools should serve rich and poor alike.[6]

Built by Communities, for Communities

The first histories of American education, which concentrate on legislation, give the impression that state assemblies, inspired by eloquent advocates like Horace Mann of Massachusetts, created the first public schools. Yet in Alabama and other states, many of the public schools were already operating *before* the legislatures acted.[7] If not the legislators, then who saw to it that future generations would have access to instruction? It turns out that public schooling wasn't just a product of democratic idealism. Most schools listed as "public" in the 1850 census were largely community institutions established for community reasons.

---

[6] Lawrence A. Cremin, *The American Common School: An Historic Conception* (New York: Bureau of Publications, Teachers College, Columbia University, 1951).

[7] Legislation creating a state system didn't pass in Maryland, for example, until 1865. Churches created many of New Jersey's schools, and they received state funding until 1838. The state system of free public schools was put into place in 1871. School legislation in Michigan authorized district schools in 1809, and in 1821, a university board of trustees was given the authority to establish a system of primary schools. But the state system didn't become a reality until Detroit turned over control of its schools in 1869.

Jon Perdue compared the founding of public schools in Alabama to those in three other states and found them similar. The sources he used are reported in "The Roots of Public Schools," *Kettering Exchange* (Fall 1999): 11-17.

In the area of Alabama I studied, citizens in community after community spurred other citizens to build, finance, staff, and operate many of the first schools. Similarly, "in the rural Northeast and the new Midwest," Carl Kaestle reported in his history of common schools, "the characteristic school was the district school, organized and controlled by a small locality."[8]

Even though legislators justified their education laws on the basis of high-minded ideals, communities had a more immediate and practical reason. They needed schools in order to survive—and their schools needed them. Community expectations gave schools what amounted to a charter with a number of mandates to carry out in conjunction with other educating institutions, like families.

These early schools were public in that the citizenry was directly involved in their operation. People built them, directed them through local trustees, and selected their teachers. The community and the school were, in many ways, one. The community wasn't just "involved" with its school, the two were inseparable. The quality of the schools was used as evidence of the character of the community. A good school was a town's proudest symbol of its public-spiritedness, a symbol used to attract new settlers and gain a competitive advantage over other towns.

Products and Agents of Self-Rule

After clearing land and putting up cabins, settlers turned to community building, which involved not only the construction of shops and streets but also the creation of a way of life reflecting their highest values. Schools were among the first institutions people established because they were a means for creating the kind of society they wanted. The schools were the handiwork of a collective citizenry.

How did pioneers find the time and energy for all this public work? They did it by using everyday activities and social occasions for political purposes. A historian of the lives of "plain folk," Frank Owsley, provided numerous examples of these occasions: Settlers gathered to build homes for newlyweds, women got together at quilting bees, neighbors assembled to clear fields by logrolling and wood-burning, and groups shucked corn to the sound of communal singing (work and

---

[8] Kaestle, *Pillars of the Republic*, p. 13.

play were often combined). All of these collective efforts built connective tissue for the frontier's civic infrastructure. They also encouraged mutual assistance and a spirit of reciprocity. They generated social capital.[9]

Politics and religion were often joined in campground revivals, which reflected the egalitarian spirit that permeated frontier politics. As Wayne Flynt showed in his study of Alabama Baptists, these gatherings affirmed the power and freedom of ordinary people and promoted a civic consciousness that advanced public education as well as other causes.[10] Camp meetings paved the way for collective activities and for more explicitly political gatherings. Newspapers frequently carried notices of public meetings. At these assemblies, people didn't just voice opinions about what others should do; they made decisions about what *they* were going to do. Their choices resulted in roads being built, businesses organized, agriculture improved, and armies raised. All were the products of people's collective power. This was self-rule in action.

Women were particularly adept at using social occasions for political purposes. Despite being excluded from voting, they participated actively in civic work, often motivated by their responsibility for nurturing the young. Early nineteenth-century women took advantage of personal relationships and social settings to organize collective responses to shared problems. They drew on what we now call networks. Wielding considerable influence in what were called the "benevolent enterprises," these women formed voluntary organizations to provide services that would later be administered by governments.[11]

---

[9] Frank Lawrence Owsley, *Plain Folk of the Old South* (1949; reprint, with an introduction by Grady McWhiney, Baton Rouge: Louisiana State University Press, 1982), pp. 90-132. Ray Oldenburg identified the modern equivalents of these gatherings in *The Great Good Place: Cafés, Coffee Shops, Bookstores, Bars, Hair Salons, and Other Hangouts at the Heart of a Community* (New York: Marlowe, 1999).

[10] Wayne Flynt, *Alabama Baptists: Southern Baptists in the Heart of Dixie* (Tuscaloosa: The University of Alabama Press, 1998), p. 52.

[11] Women's role in shaping social policy was one of the subjects of Sara M. Evans' *Born for Liberty: A History of Women in America* (New York: Free Press, 1989). John W. Quist dealt with the role of women in social reform in *Restless Visionaries: The Social Roots of Antebellum Reform in Alabama and Michigan* (Baton Rouge: Louisiana State University Press, 1998), pp. 198-199.

Today, when people consider doing something political, they want to know where to begin. The women of the nineteenth century would tell them to start where they are—to begin where they did, in the places people normally congregate. That would certainly be sound advice for leaders of community organizations and educators who are having difficulty getting a crowd to turn out for their meetings. Maybe they should go where people already gather.

Almost everything people did in education could be traced back to a handful of people sitting around someone's kitchen table. These small, independent initiatives weren't necessarily connected through formal organizations, but they resonated with one another and influenced the overall political climate. By the mid-nineteenth century, legislators had gotten the message. They knew that communities had done as much as they could for the general diffusion of knowledge and wanted their state government to do its part.

I don't mean to imply that antebellum pioneers had such a vibrant civic life that they created a golden age of education. The people who lived then would be the last to say that.

Schools and Social Justice

Although citizens had practical reasons for wanting schools, they weren't purely pragmatic. Ideals simply took on a different form in communities. "Justice," for instance, was understood as fairness and an absence of privilege.

I learned about the importance of social justice from David Chapman Mathews, my grandfather, who was a county superintendent during the 1920s. At the time, differences in educational opportunity were dividing our county (Clarke). Schools attended by black youngsters had few resources, and those for whites offered vastly disparate kinds of education. Some towns provided a full nine months of instruction, while in rural areas, schools operated for only five. The difference promoted class distinctions, even though children attending the two types of schools were often related to one another. My grandfather explained that "one brother might live in Grove Hill and own a store. His children would get to go to school for nine months. His brother might live across the creek on a farm, and his children would get only five months of schooling." This offended my grandfather's sense of fairness: "Coming from the country or rural area, naturally,

25

my sympathies were with the country child. I despised the disparity; it was un-American, undemocratic, and not Christian to have such a distinction."[12] (In 1922, the citizens of the county voted overwhelmingly to increase their school taxes, which reduced some of the inequity.)

Schools without the Public

Given the tradition of citizens working with citizens and citizens working with schools, how did America get to the point where people would say the public schools "aren't ours"? The trend to disenfranchise the very people who created the first schools, as evident in Alabama, has been reported in national studies as well.[13] In 1854, Alabama committed itself to a comprehensive system of public education, which was supported by large majorities in both houses of the legislature. Political leaders at the time said that the vote was brought about by a citizenry "alive to the importance of education."[14] Tragically, soon after the Alabama legislature adjourned, the public and the public schools began to drift apart. In a relatively short period of time, the community-based citizenry that had established the schools began to lose some of its control to the state government—and, with it, some of its sense of responsibility.

The first state superintendent of education, William Perry, recognized that the public had been responsible for the legislative victory in 1854 and, upon taking office, described himself as the servant of the people. Not long after, however, Perry was busy rewriting his job description, a revision that Perry's successor, Gabriel DuVal, endorsed. Rather than rallying citizens as compatriots in a

---

[12] My grandfather made a series of recordings for his grandchildren in the 1970s, which include the story of the struggle to provide children in rural areas with the same nine months of schooling that children in the towns were receiving. These recordings and a transcript of them titled "Children's Stories" are at the Clarke County Historical Society in Grove Hill, Alabama.

[13] Kaestle, *Pillars of the Republic*; David Tyack and Elizabeth Hansot, *Managers of Virtue: Public School Leadership in America, 1820-1980* (New York: Basic Books, 1982); and David Tyack and Larry Cuban, *Tinkering toward Utopia: A Century of Public School Reform* (Cambridge, MA: Harvard University Press, 1995).

[14] Alabama House of Representatives, *Report from the Committee on Education, on the Subject of Public Schools* (Montgomery: Brittan and De Wolf, 1852), pp. 5, 10.

common cause, the superintendents came to describe their mission as persuading the ignorant and indifferent.[15]

Reforms advocated by Perry and DuVal struck at the core of local control, and communities resisted. The silver bullet for progress in Perry's eyes was instruction that conformed to supposedly universal principles. A nationwide romance with a surefire "science" of education so captivated him that he established the state's first standards for schools. Professional administrators in the capital, rather than local trustees, were to select the subjects to be taught and the texts to be used. The justification for the change, according to state officials, was that local boards were filled with "plain unlettered men" who weren't qualified to make sound educational decisions.[16]

Perry was only following in the footsteps of superintendents across the country when he imposed state standards. And he didn't want his actions to give Alabamians the impression that the state government was assuming full responsibility for schooling. He said so explicitly. In time, however, his worst fears would be realized. Historians David Tyack and Elizabeth Hansot have shown how "the rise of expertise in management gradually eroded an earlier common ground of support for the common school" across the country.[17] William Perry was not an exception to the rule; he was the rule personified.

---

[15] The duties of the state superintendent of education and the way the first two men who held that office understood their duties—along with the reforms they proposed—are in the following documents: William F. Perry, *Report of the Superintendent of Education of the State of Alabama, to the Governor* (Montgomery: Brittan and Blue, 1855); *Annual Report of William F. Perry, Superintendent of Education, of the State of Alabama, Made to the Governor, for the Year 1856* (Montgomery: Smith and Hughes, 1857); *Report of William F. Perry, Superintendent of Education, of the State of Alabama, Made to the Governor, for the Year 1857* (Montgomery: N. B. Cloud, 1858); William F. Perry, "The Genesis of Public Education in Alabama," in *Transactions of the Alabama Historical Society: 1897-1898*, ed. Thomas McAdory Owen, vol. 2 (Tuscaloosa: Alabama Historical Society, 1898); and *Report of Gabriel B. DuVal, Superintendent of Education, of the State of Alabama, Made to the Governor, for the Year 1858* (Montgomery: Shorter and Reid, 1859).

[16] William F. Perry told of his efforts to deal with county and township officials in "Genesis of Public Education," p. 20 and *Report of William F. Perry, 1857*, pp. 12-16. The amended school law was in Alabama General Assembly, *Acts*, 5th biennial sess., 1855-1856 (Montgomery: Bates and Lucas, 1856), pp. 33-48.

[17] Tyack and Hansot, *Managers of Virtue*, p. 13.

By 1904, Alabama was facing a serious literacy crisis. Illiteracy soared to the highest levels in the country. A group of concerned citizens, including leading educators and a former governor, insisted that the only remedy was to restore local ownership of schools. Pride in the schools had faded away, they argued, because citizens had little voice in matters of education. Furthermore, a new constitution adopted in 1901 limited the amount of tax money counties could raise, so Alabamians couldn't do much at the local level to solve their problems. One leading citizen warned that "a democratic government pursues a suicidal policy when it declares the people incompetent to decide for themselves."[18]

To be sure, centralization at the state level was never absolute; local boards and savvy county superintendents quickly learned how to retain a considerable amount of power. Yet public ownership of schools and the sense of community responsibility that went with it were eroding. Schools that citizens had built were in danger of turning into schools citizens could scarcely affect. And the public, once grounded in self-rule, was on its way to becoming a public without the ground needed to rule itself.

Across the country, local school boards of "plain unlettered men" continued to be an inviting target for reform-minded educators. Nicholas Murray Butler, president of Columbia University, argued vociferously that the schools didn't really belong to the public but to their administrators. In a curious bit of reasoning, he insisted that "a democracy is as much entitled as a monarchy to have its business well done." Butler believed that "the less the personal contact between the voter and public candidate, the greater the chance of an efficient appointed board," and he disparaged "the local-committee system of school government" as the worst system that had "ever been invented by man."[19]

The Columbia president was typical of the professional elites who arrived on the scene at the turn of the twentieth century. They wanted

[18] John Herbert Phillips, "Local Taxation for Schools," in *Local Taxation for Schools in Alabama* (Montgomery: Phillips-Sheehan, n.d.), p. 16.

[19] Nicholas Murray Butler, "Remarks of Dr. Butler, President of Columbia University, before the Merchants' Club, on Saturday, December 8th, at the Auditorium," in *Public Schools and Their Administration: Addresses Delivered at the Fifty-ninth Meeting of the Merchants' Club of Chicago* (Chicago: Merchants' Club, 1906), pp. 40, 42, 47.

to reshape "the schools according to canons of business efficiency and scientific expertise." Rather than mobilizing local citizens to act, they were determined to take schools out of politics. Their efforts were, nonetheless, intensely political because they were certain about who should govern and how they should govern. Local boards made up of citizens were increasingly challenged by "successful men" who advocated a more centralized system of governance led by professionals. Large cities discontinued ward boards, and membership on other boards declined to a select few. The number of school trustees dropped even more sharply as administrators took over more duties and schools were consolidated.[20]

I am not suggesting that arguments like Butler's by themselves resulted in administrators having greater control of the schools. Still, the uncritical embrace of purported scientific certainty in matters of education and management built walls that shut out citizens. Inherently political issues in the educational debate became masked as scientific and technical considerations, which were not considered to be in the public's province.

This isn't to say that local authority for schools has always served the public's interest and that professional control has done just the opposite. As Tyack and Hansot have explained:

> Simply arguing that the "community" should "control" its schools ignores the many ways in which local decision makers have been able to use schools to perpetuate racial, class, religious, and sexual discrimination. To claim that "experts" know best or that state or federal governments have the wisdom to decree a "one best system" is not only arrogant—it also disregards the checkered recent history of instructional "reforms" imposed from without.[21]

During the latter half of the twentieth century, centralization continued, despite attempts to restore local control. After the Supreme Court decision in the *Brown* case in 1954, opponents of school integration used local jurisdiction as an argument to contest federal intervention, which discredited community boards and reduced their authority even more. Yet, in this same period, local groups of citizens

---

[20] Tyack and Hansot, *Managers of Virtue*, pp. 106-107. Also see Tyack and Cuban, *Tinkering toward Utopia*.

[21] Tyack and Hansot, *Managers of Virtue*, p. 253.

(often ad hoc) were sometimes a decisive force in bringing about peaceful integration. In cities from Dallas, Texas, to Pontiac, Michigan, people formed coalitions across racial divides to rally support for the public schools. In 1976, the Ford administration attempted, unsuccessfully, to get Congress to recognize the constructive role this citizenry was playing by proposing a national commission to assist them. And former HEW Secretary Arthur Flemming urged the Carter administration to create a "National Citizens Committee for the Desegregation of the Nation's Schools." Flemming, too, was unsuccessful.[22] The federal courts, however, used biracial committees in carrying out desegregation orders.[23]

After integration became less of a crisis, many of these local biracial groups faded away, and few communities recalled their important role when the schools faced new challenges at the end of the twentieth century. Contributing to this decline in civic capacity, some organizations that had been instrumental in forming local civic associations decided that organizing citizens community by community was less cost effective than lobbying in Washington.[24]

---

[22] The national commission was to be the National Community and Education Commission, recommended by HEW and created by executive order. Lawrence J. McAndrews, "Missing the Bus: Gerald Ford and School Desegregation," *Presidential Studies Quarterly* 27 (Fall 1997): 791-804.

Arthur Flemming offered the National Citizens Committee for the Desegregation of the Nation's Schools while he was chair of the U.S. Commission on Civil Rights. Dean J. Kotlowski, *Nixon's Civil Rights: Politics, Principle, and Policy* (Cambridge, MA: Harvard University Press, 2001), p. 43.

[23] The call for "biracial communities" seems to have come out of the early civil rights movement. For instance, it was one of the demands Martin Luther King Jr. made in Birmingham, Alabama. Diane McWhorter, *Carry Me Home: Birmingham, Alabama, The Climactic Battle of the Civil Rights Revolution* (New York: Simon and Schuster, 2001), p. 381.

My assessment of biracial groups comes from personal experience. I thought they provided essential public space for working on integration. Another assessment can be found in Marilyn J. Gittell's *Limits to Citizen Participation: The Decline of Community Organizations* (Beverly Hills: Sage Publications, 1980).

[24] Two scholars who have found an erosion in civic life are Theda Skocpol and Robert Putnam, who argued that Americans were "bowling alone." Theda Skocpol, *Diminished Democracy: From Membership to Management in American Civic Life* (Norman: University of Oklahoma Press, 2003) and Robert D. Putnam, *Bowling Alone: The Collapse and Revival of American Community* (New York: Simon and Schuster, 2000).

This change in the strategy of national organizations reduced opportunities for citizens to decide and act together. The public became a less potent political force.

At the same time, especially after 1960, the scope and degree of federal involvement increased substantially, affecting nearly every aspect of community life. Despite more programs and expanded benefits, however, governments in general and the federal government in particular, began to lose legitimacy in the eyes of many citizens. Stung by the Watergate scandal and frustrated by the war in Vietnam, people's confidence in all major institutions fell in the 1970s and continued to fall. Attempts to open governments through various citizen participation initiatives had no discernable effect on citizens' feelings of being shut out of a political system. The ties between the public and the public schools became even more strained.[25]

The next chapter continues and expands the analysis of the forces that have kept citizens on the sidelines of schools. The absence of a public for public schools was particularly evident in the attempts at school reform in the 1980s and 1990s. Americans care deeply about education, but many of these reform initiatives, though undertaken in their interest, gave little more than lip service to citizen participation.

---

[25] To learn more about the loss of public confidence in government, see Steven M. Gillon, *"That's Not What We Meant to Do": Reform and Its Unintended Consequences in Twentieth-Century America* (New York: Norton, 2000); Joseph S. Nye Jr., "Introduction: The Decline of Confidence in Government," in *Why People Don't Trust Government*, ed. Joseph S. Nye Jr., Philip D. Zelikow, and David C. King (Cambridge, MA: Harvard University Press, 1997); David Brian Robertson, ed., *Loss of Confidence: Politics and Policy in the 1970s* (University Park: Pennsylvania State University Press, 1998); and Bruce J. Schulman, *The Seventies: The Great Shift in American Culture, Society, and Politics* (New York: Free Press, 2001).

CHAPTER THREE
THE RELATIONSHIP WE HAVE/ THE RELATIONSHIP WE WANT

Neither the ideals of the nineteenth-century common school movement nor the sensibilities of frontier communities about the value of public instruction have completely disappeared. Recapping a bit of what was said in the first chapter, people want public schools because of tradition and because of the importance they place on giving all youngsters an opportunity to better themselves, irrespective of their financial circumstances. Americans are genuinely troubled about what would happen if the country turned away from these institutions, despite headlines questioning their value. As a man in Boston asked rhetorically, "If you didn't have public schools where would the children go if they couldn't afford to go to private school?"[1]

Citizens are especially opposed to school policies that would widen the gap between haves and have-nots, so they hesitate to let market forces have full sway. Americans worry about any policy that would result in the rich getting richer and the poor getting poorer. They are well aware that the public schools have been one of the few institutions where children from different backgrounds can come together. That realization, more than anything else, sustains support for public education.[2]

At the same time, the ambivalence about the schools noted in the first chapter remains. A good many people seem to be saying, in effect, "We should have public schools, but we don't want to send our kids there—and you shouldn't either." Even some who would benefit from a level playing field feel trapped in today's schools. "Low income people can't move," explained a woman in Chicago; "We're in such a helpless situation," a Boston woman lamented.[3] If the public schools

---

[1] The Harwood Group, *Halfway out the Door: Citizens Talk about Their Mandate for Public Schools* (Dayton, OH: Report to the Kettering Foundation, 1995), p. 4.

[2] Ibid., p. 5.

[3] Ibid., pp. 13-15.

become the last refuge for children who have nowhere else to go, then America will end up with a very different kind of school system from the one we have had historically.

Despite frustrations on both sides of the divide between the public and the public schools, I am convinced that enough political will could be generated to bridge the gap. Citizens don't want to sit on the sidelines of public education. I accept the findings that Americans are eager to work with educators but want a relationship among equals. Using an analogy from business, a woman from Massachusetts explained: "It's just like in a lot of industries. Where I work we're in what they call the team concept and our business is running much better than it ever did when we had a hierarchy." A man in Maryland made a similar point: "If we let the grassroots do more work I think we'd be in good shape."[4]

Wary educators don't always warm to such assistance because they fear citizens will invade their turf. An irate parent or special interest group might well try to step over the line. But professionals need not be so wary. As reported in Chapter 1, the citizenry as a whole doesn't want to take over running the schools. A study of parents, who might be the most likely to want to micromanage the schools, found that they aren't power hungry. Few want to take over administrative responsibilities or teach math.[5] A group of citizens in West Virginia went further in distinguishing the role of professionals from their own role. Even though mindful of the expertise teachers bring to the classroom, they were reluctant to "leave it to the professionals" to make every decision about education. These West Virginians thought that a community's collective judgment was better on some issues. Treating education as a purely professional matter, they said, "widens the gulf between the public and its schools."[6]

---

[4] Ibid., p. 19.

[5] Public Agenda, *Playing Their Parts: Parents and Teachers Talk about Parental Involvement in Public Schools* (New York: Public Agenda, 1999), pp. 12-13.

[6] West Virginia Center for Civic Life, *Ties That Bind: West Virginians Talk about Their Relationship with Public Schools* (Charleston: West Virginia Center for Civic Life, October 2000), pp. 6-7.

The tension between professional educators and the public is longstanding and is documented in David Tyack and Elisabeth Hansot, *Managers of Virtue: Public School Leadership in America, 1820-1980* (New York: Basic Books, 1982), p. 226. The authors reported that administrators were taught that they, not outside pressure groups, should set school policy. Their training did not develop the "ability to hear or persuade a pluralistic public."

A Legacy of Distrust

The attitudes in West Virginia about professionals may reflect the distrust that built up in the 1980s and 1990s when reformers set out to sell their proposals to improve the schools. Many of those proposals were probably worth considering, and they were offered with the best of intentions. Yet they left a legacy of distrust that has grown to the point of developing its own grassroots. The reforms were usually based on an implicit assumption that improvements would come primarily from school administrators, who would be supported by influential business and civic leaders. Later, on reflection, some reformers recognized what had gone wrong. Communities had been ignored. As one experienced administrator testified, "you can't do school reform inside the school."[7]

In spite of initial bursts of optimism and abundant promises, many reform efforts became "divided within and besieged without."[8] A study by Public Agenda found that the key actors in reforms (educators, parents, business leaders, board members) were unable to overcome sharp differences over goals. Trapped in a web of suspicion, extreme partisanship, competitiveness, and poor communication, the leading participants became the leading combatants, unable to reach any common ground. Turf battles emerged every time a proposal threatened someone's domain. Even those closest to the school system resorted to adversarial tactics. Parents, who might be expected to have an interest in the overall quality of education, besieged the schools in order to win personal concessions rather than bring about systemic change.

Investigating these reform initiatives for the *Washington Monthly*, Katherine Boo found that when they floundered, the failure disillusioned the communities that had undertaken them. Boo discovered one common problem: While the specific proposals might have been technically sound, the reformers were unable to master the process of

---

[7] Reported by Ann Hallett, Kettering Foundation meeting, minutes, April 13, 1995, Kettering Foundation, Dayton, OH, p. 3.

[8] Of course, reforms don't all fail. The problem is that we don't seem to know how to sustain successes or move them from one school or area to another. Many successful reforms die when those who initiated them move on. Trying to imitate successful models doesn't seem to work. Steve Farkas with Jean Johnson, *Divided Within, Besieged Without: The Politics of Education in Four American School Districts* (New York: Public Agenda Report to the Kettering Foundation, 1993).

change.[9] In paying understandable attention to *what* they were going to change, they neglected the question of *how* to put the changes in place.

The reformers Boo wrote about didn't normally involve parents, let alone community members. Paying lip service to the notion of citizen participation, most worked "doggedly to keep the masses from messing with their plans."[10] Consequently, the public didn't have a seat at the table, and there wasn't a citizenry available to relate particular interests to the larger community interests or bring about a measure of accommodation among the principal stakeholders. There were exceptions, of course. In Kentucky, reformers organized forums across the state, not to advocate a predetermined plan, but to listen to what citizens had to say.[11]

For the most part, the reform campaigns operated as though the longstanding commitment to public schools was still intact and that educators only had to demonstrate legitimate needs in order for taxpayers to provide funds. The key actors tried to rally people through the standard means of publicity and marketing, treating citizens as though they were consumers waiting to be told the benefits of the reformers' "products." Apparently, leaders of these campaigns thought that any disagreements between school officials and the citizenry could be settled through more effective communication.[12] There was little in most reform efforts to suggest that the public was anything more than an audience to be reached or that citizens had anything to do other than give their consent to a plan.

Keeping Citizens on the Sidelines

If these were the reformers' assumptions, they were mistaken. People found what reformers were saying either incoherent, irrelevant, or both. Key actors talked about discrete policy solutions and funding

---

[9] Katherine Boo, "Reform School Confidential: What We Can Learn for Three of America's Boldest School Reforms," *Washington Monthly* 24 (October 1992): 17-24.

[10] Ibid., p. 24.

[11] Robert F. Sexton, *Mobilizing Citizens for Better Schools* (New York: Teachers College Press, 2004).

[12] Strategies to present a better image for the schools and communicate more effectively with citizens were eventually joined by strategies to engage citizens on their own terms. By 1998, the National School Public Relations Association was advocating public deliberations on school issues for that purpose.

issues that didn't connect with people's everyday concerns. And when reform leaders argued among themselves and pointed fingers, citizens decided the combatants were locked into a debate that lacked any promise of real change. Making matters worse, educators often responded to questions in a technical language, which made people asking the questions feel they weren't being heard. Citizens said, in effect, "We are over here with the problems; the school reformers are over there with their solutions."[13]

Even people with concerns that might have been directly affected by proposed reforms (parents, for example) felt excluded because, as they saw it, their participation wasn't really valued by professionals. A survey done in the 1990s showed that this perception wasn't baseless. Nearly 60 percent of Americans thought parents and other members of the community should have more say in allocating funds and setting curricular priorities. Only 26 percent of teachers and less than 15 percent of administrators agreed.[14] Perhaps sensing this disparity, superintendents began having more conversations with citizens at open house days in the schools and meeting more often with volunteers. These were commendable attempts at outreach, but the assumptions about the public never changed. The public was a citizenry to be assigned tasks from agendas set by professionals.[15]

Because the reforms had no plans for meaningful work by citizens, people didn't believe they could do much to bring about the changes they wanted. What they were often asked to do for schools—holding bake sales or volunteering as aides—didn't seem capable of making a real difference. Other citizens just stayed away from the schools and expressed their frustration in comments like, "I wouldn't know how to be involved . . . I really wouldn't." At best, people thought they might help a particular child or a few children through their own individual

---

[13] The Harwood Group, *How Citizens View Education: Their Public Concerns and Private Actions* (Dayton, OH: Report to the Kettering Foundation, 1993) and Doble Research Associates, *Education and the Public: Summaries of Five Research Projects* (Dayton, OH: Report to the Kettering Foundation, March 1996), pp. 17-19.

[14] Steve Farkas, *Educational Reform: The Players and the Politics* (Dayton, OH: Public Agenda Report to the Kettering Foundation, 1992), p. 18.

[15] Public Agenda, *Just Waiting to Be Asked: A Fresh Look at Attitudes on Public Engagement* (New York: Public Agenda, 2001), pp. 22-24.

efforts; they saw little opportunity for collective action.[16] Recall that when people consider investing their time, they want some assurance that their investment will make a difference. If they don't get that assurance—if they can't find anything meaningful to get their hands on—they lose interest. Getting our hands on a problem prompts a sense that we *might* make a difference; we don't expect that everything we do will be successful, but improvement becomes imaginable.[17]

In contrast to reformers, who had high hopes that the schools would change, citizens were skeptical. Many considered school systems black holes: Any money the schools were given would disappear because of inefficient management. "The schools are run by a bloated, overpaid, out-of-touch bureaucracy that is accountable to no one," a man from Baton Rouge fumed. In agreement, a neighbor said flatly that while the schools need more revenue, he would oppose a referendum to raise taxes because the money "will only be wasted by a system the community doesn't control." In Tulsa, Oklahoma, comments were similar: "We don't run the schools anymore—the government does. People have not been allowed to give their input into the [educational] process because we've been suppressed." When citizens are reminded that they have the power to elect the school board, they aren't encouraged. In the Baton Rouge conversation, a woman pointed out: "What's important is who gets on the ballot in the first place. And when it comes to that, the people are powerless."[18]

Not all Americans doubted the ability of the schools to do a better job or their ability to bring about constructive change. Yet those who did were deeply pessimistic. They couldn't "conceive of *any* reform effort, no matter how well designed or intentioned, that will have a lasting, positive impact."[19]

---

[16] The Harwood Group, *How Citizens View Education*, pp. 30-31.

[17] The Harwood Group, *Meaningful Chaos: How People Form Relationships with Public Concerns* (Dayton, OH: Kettering Foundation, 1993). Also see Doble Research Associates, *A Consumer Mentality: The Prevailing Mind-Set in American Public Education* (Dayton, OH: Report to the Kettering Foundation, 1999), p. 15.

[18] Doble Research Associates, *The Comprehensive Educational Resources Inventory: An Analytic Summary of the Results from the CERI Research* (Dayton, OH: Report to the Kettering Foundation, 1994), p. 3.

[19] Ibid., p. 3.

Some reform efforts in the 1980s and 1990s did overcome this cynicism. It happened in statewide political campaigns in which explicit measures to improve schools were included in proposals to raise taxes. In Mississippi, Governor William Winter faced a state assembly in 1981 that was dead set against raising taxes. So, in 1982, he revived the campaign strategy he had used to win office and launched old-fashioned rallies across the state. Winter went directly to the people—and he won. The legislature got the message, and the schools received a large increase in revenue. Other governors followed Winter's example: Richard Riley in South Carolina, Bill Clinton in Arkansas (in his second term), Lamar Alexander in Tennessee, and Chuck Robb in Virginia. In fact, virtually every governor in the region made education a significant part of his agenda.[20]

The Ideal: "My Kids Are Going to an Excellent School, and I'm Involved with It"

Americans who are not pessimistic about the public schools are usually doing something to contribute to the education of children. Interestingly, private schools provide some of the best examples of what citizens can do to get off the sidelines. The attraction of private schools is telling. Whether true or not, Americans imagine them to be what public schools should be, but aren't.[21] According to surveys, one of the most appealing qualities of these schools isn't high academic standards or order. It is the relationship between these schools and

---

[20] Ken Barr at Kettering reviewed the literature on these public education campaigns in the South, which actually date back to efforts by governors like Reubin Askew of Florida and John West of South Carolina, who built citizen coalitions to generate support for school integration. See Andrew P. Mullins Jr., *Building Consensus: A History of the Passage of the Mississippi Education Reform Act of 1982* (1992); Gordon E. Harvey, *A Question of Justice: New South Governors and Education, 1968-1976* (Tuscaloosa: The University of Alabama Press, 2002); and Jennie Vanetta Carter Thomas, "How Three Governors Involved the Public in Passing Their Education Reform Programs" (EdD diss., George Peabody College for Teachers of Vanderbilt University, 1992).

[21] Public Agenda, *On Thin Ice: How Advocates and Opponents Could Misread the Public's Views on Vouchers and Charter Schools* (New York: Public Agenda, 1999), p. 13.

their constituents. Parents, grandparents, alumni, even the parents of alumni, are encouraged to become involved in the life of these schools.[22]

The public schools given high marks are those that have cultivated similar relationships with parents and members of the community. People who speak well of their school tend to add that what they like most is their close association with it. Taking part in the life of a school seems to be linked to a perception that the school is a good one. As one person testified when asked why he was pleased with the local public schools, "[My kids] are going to an excellent school, and I'm involved with it."[23] "I'm involved" can be the first step toward "we are involved" and the relational accountability that I discussed earlier.

Unfortunately, many parents of public school students aren't involved, even though some would very much like to be.[24] The mother of a sixth grader told of her frustration when she couldn't have lunch with her child occasionally or deliver a message during recess. When others hear stories like this, they are apt to recall a time when children

---

[22] The notion that public schools have to be changed or reformed has been around as long as there have been schools. They are so central to nearly every national and local objective that it is probably inevitable that we always want to reshape them. That said, it is sad that we have reached a point in the United States where these institutions are considered the least responsive to pressures to change, even though people without and within have tried to solve the mysteries of organizational reform. When water is blocked at one point, it finds another route, and something like that appears to be happening in America today with the creation of alternate forms of schooling. Often established institutions have changed, not by internal reorganization but by absorbing or creating their own versions of the alternatives. The political system, for example, responded to reform initiatives like popular referenda and recall elections by incorporating them. Perhaps something like this will happen in education in the twenty-first century.

[23] The Harwood Group, *Halfway out the Door*, p. 14. For more on the effects of relationships on perceptions, see Ernest G. S. Noack, "The Satisfaction of Parents with Their Community Schools as a Measure of Effectiveness of the Decentralization of a School System," *Journal of Educational Research* 65 (April 1972): 355-356.

[24] This is not to deny that many people, particularly parents, are deeply involved with the public schools as volunteers. Yet even the highly active parents give themselves low marks for their participation in the life of the school, as contrasted with their efforts in connection with their children's homework. See Institute for Educational Leadership, *Survey of Parent Involvement* (Washington, DC: Institute for Educational Leadership, 1995).

were conscious of being on their best behavior because they knew their parents were welcome to drop by the school at any time—and often did.

In their defense, educators aren't necessarily being inhospitable. Bad experiences have made them reluctant to open their doors, and their caution has been reinforced by the need to keep students safe. Whatever the reasons, lack of hallway contact between citizens (not just parents) and the schools may go a long way in explaining why their relationship has soured.

People Talk about Their Relationship with the Schools

Because the kind of relationship people have with schools is so important, Kettering decided to learn more about it. The objective of this research wasn't to find out how to improve relationships so people would feel better about schools or educators would feel better about citizens. The purpose was to gain a better understanding of what it might take to restore public ownership. The foundation discovered that people had at least five quite distinct ways of describing how they related to schools.[25]

Inattentives

Some of those interviewed for the research said they had absolutely no relationship with the public schools—and didn't want one. Schools weren't on their radar screens. It will come as no surprise that many of these "inattentives" were retirees or people whose children were no longer in school. Others were single adults who had no children, and a few (and this was surprising) were young married couples. Recall that Americans with school-age youngsters amount to only about one-third of the population (depending on the locality), so the number of inattentives can be sizable in certain communities.

Dropouts

A second group consisted of people who had left the system, preferring to send their children to private schools or to educate them at home. Although they had no relationship with the public schools,

---

[25] My description of inattentives, dropouts, and shutouts was drawn from Doble Research Associates, *How People Connect: The Public and Public Schools* (Dayton, OH: Report to the Kettering Foundation, June 1998).

some were still worried about the quality of public education because it affects everything from their property values to the community's economic competitiveness. For instance, a physician might send his children to a private school and, in that sense, be a dropout. At the same time, he might also be interested in the public schools because he realizes that he can't recruit new doctors to his practice if these schools aren't up to par.

Shutouts

Some people very much wanted to have a close relationship with the schools yet were frustrated to the point of anger because they couldn't find a way in. Here are more complaints similar to those I quoted earlier: "I tried to get into my child's school, and it was as if it were locked." And, "When I was a child, it was not uncommon to see my mother, my father, and my neighbors in the hallway; now there's a guard."[26] Ironically, parents' days or open houses may only underscore the perception that being in the school isn't the norm.

Complaints about not being welcome in the schools have come up time and again in Kettering research. Educators counter with cases where citizens—even parents—have not responded, even when urged to become involved in their children's schooling. An advocate for parents summed up the difference in perceptions this way: "Schools feel that they're doing a lot to get parents involved, and parents feel that they aren't doing enough."[27] Is one group or the other wrong? Or does the difference have more to do with perceptions of roles? Professionals

---

[26] Studies other than the one done by Doble report this same perception of being shut out. A report on family partnerships with high schools found, "Over 90 percent of the parents surveyed agreed that parent involvement was needed at the high school level. . . . Few parents reported being involved in school activities such as volunteering, fund raising, or committee participation. However, 75% of the parents reported that the school had never contacted them about such activities and felt that such contact was important for their teens' school success." Mavis G. Sanders, Joyce L. Epstein, and Lori Connors-Tadros, *Family Partnerships with High Schools: The Parents' Perspective* (Center for Research on the Education of Students Placed at Risk, February 1999), p. 4.

[27] Bryan Goodwin and Sheila A. Arens, *No Community Left Behind? An Analysis of the Potential Impact of the No Child Left Behind Act of 2001 on School-Community Relationships* (Dayton, OH: McREL Report to the Kettering Foundation, May 2003), p. 26.

may not share citizens' ideas about their role and vice versa. Whatever the cause, the disparity in perceptions indicates a relationship in trouble.

Consumers

The largest group of people in the study described themselves as customers or consumers of educational services. They wanted to drop their children off at 8:00 AM and return at 3:00 PM, expecting the youngsters to have received the instruction the parents had paid for with their taxes. Consumers said their job was to watch educators the way they watch a "cashier making change." Their children sometimes adopted their parents' point of view, thinking that they should help "keep the school in line."[28]

Classroom teachers are quick to feel the effects of this attitude. They complain that educating children is doubly difficult if it is seen as solely their responsibility. I recall a teacher saying that if parents worked with him in carrying out a shared responsibility for their children, he could do a pretty good job. If they didn't, he feared that neither his experience nor his skill would be equal to the task. Demonstrating that not all teachers are averse to having "outsiders" in the classroom, he wanted parents to join him. Professionals with his mindset struggle mightily to promote shared responsibility, pressing their colleagues to do the same.[29]

Consumers appeared more concerned about their individual rights than they were about the well-being of their community. As a woman from Dayton said, "No one thinks of community anymore. Everyone's

---

[28] The attitude of parents as consumers was described in Doble Research Associates, *A Consumer Mentality*, pp. 2, 9-10.

[29] "Struggle" is not an empty term, as Tenney Hammond explained in an e-mail to the foundation. Tenney teaches in the Cleveland schools and doesn't think she can empower her students by herself. She set out to build the notion of shared responsibility into her professional relationships. Doing forums with other teachers seemed like a good idea, but there was too much material to cover on the "district pacing calendar" to add them. Her proposal to reach out beyond the school to involve nonprofessionals met with assurances that attendance at sports events and community use of school facilities were sufficient evidence of engagement. Parental involvement seemed to be something that would appeal to both educators and citizens, yet in the meetings "everything was aimed at teachers," and parents weren't interested in the topics on the agenda—instructional and communications models. Tenney Hammond, e-mail message to Connie Crockett, July 13, 2004.

thinking about individual rights, who they're going to sue."[30] She shared the widespread perception that America is suffering from a breakdown of its communities. When people doubt that neighbors care about neighbors or look out for other people's children, they tend to look out for themselves. This perception becomes self-confirming and promotes consumerism.

Interestingly, consumers didn't always consider theirs to be the ideal relationship with the schools. Yet acting as a consumer has worked, and administrators seemed to encourage it. Other people really liked the idea of being consumers and resisted any suggestion that consumer-oriented behavior contributed to the problems they complained about. Not to insist on good service, they argued, would relieve schools of their obligation to do a good job.[31]

Those who think of themselves as consumers are ambivalent about the "producers," that is, the public schools. They have about as many complaints as compliments. So, any assumption that treating parents and taxpayers as consumers will make them happier is suspect. In the end, even if acting like a shopper does result in better service from the schools, it won't lead to public ownership or encourage collective responsibility. As said in the Introduction, the widespread appeal of consumerism suggests a decided lack of public ownership.

Partners

The last group identified in the study was numerically small but substantively quite significant. People in this group wanted to take their share of responsibility for young people and did, through a variety of collaborative projects. They were the only ones with a consistently positive view of the public schools. They considered these institutions their agents, not only in educating children *but also in improving their communities.* The schools had dual purposes, and improving the community attracted people who weren't parents because they believed that "the well-being of their community is inextricably linked to what goes on in the schools."[32] Partners were more likely to be involved with the schools and probably more likely to join other citizens in collective actions to deal with the community problems that affect young people.

---

[30] Doble Research Associates, *Education and the Public*, p. 11.

[31] Doble Research Associates, *A Consumer Mentality*, pp. 12-13, 17-18, 29-30.

[32] Doble Research Associates, *How People Connect*, p. 5.

Partners as Owners

Partners seem to own their schools, perhaps because they consider them to be the hub of community life and not just instructional centers. A Paul Werth study compared the school-community connection in two cities. In City A, citizens talked like consumers, not owners. They didn't use "we" when talking about the city and had difficulty identifying the community they felt a part of. Most were concerned about the schooling of their own children, not necessarily all children. Residents described the schools as service providers and liked having the option of taking their children out of schools that weren't giving good service. There was little thought of mobilizing citizens to shore up schools that were in trouble. At most, people thought the problems of schools could be solved by giving more authority to onsite administrators. They didn't usually talk about partnerships with the schools, but those who did mentioned businesses providing financial support.[33]

City B had once been at the center of a controversy over court-ordered busing, and the subsequent work that had gone into improving race relations may have been one of the reasons residents frequently referred to themselves as "we." Citizens identified both with the city as a whole and with their neighborhood. Researchers found that people's sense of responsibility tended to transcend their obligations to their own children. They talked about the need to be involved in improving education. And more than just talking, parents and nonparents alike participated in tutorial projects as well as a technology club that taught students how to use computers. Employees of a local bank were given four hours off a month for such projects. As you might imagine, a few people in City B had the same consumeristic orientation found in City A. Most saw the schools as more than an educational service provider, and considered them "partners in addressing other community issues."[34]

The people who talked about addressing community issues probably didn't mean that they wanted the schools to assume more community responsibilities. Even though partners see the schools as important to the community, they are usually opposed to schools

---

[33] Paul Werth Associates, *Final Report* (Dayton, OH: Report to the Kettering Foundation, May 5, 2003).

[34] Ibid., p. 9.

taking on projects that would interfere with their primary mission. They just want what happens in the schools to be attuned to what the community considers valuable—attuned to the kind of society citizens want to create.

The partners in City B not only owned their schools, but also translated their ownership into a sense of public accountability. Residents weren't complacent about weakness in the educational system, but neither were they prone to place the blame on professionals. In City A, on the other hand, people seemed content to leave educators with the responsibility for the schools, though they were "quick to criticize or point out the faults."[35]

The implications of this study are fairly obvious. The more the schools are seen as community institutions, the more people believe that the schools are theirs and "with them." And from a democratic perspective, the more people are involved in collective actions to benefit the schools and the community, the stronger the public.

The Latent Community Connection

These findings suggest that more citizens would move off the sidelines if efforts to bridge the school-community divide started on the community side of the gap. Starting with what a community considers valuable might attract those who would otherwise have little relationship with the schools. There is just one problem. Most people don't instinctively turn to the schools when they think about solving community problems. Making that connection comes after some reflection—or a crisis. Only those who think of themselves as partners start with the assumption that the school is the hub of the community.

In 1995, research done for Kettering showed that Americans believed the public schools existed solely to prepare children for the future. Individual success was the goal, not community or social well-being. The purpose of schooling, interviewees explained, is "to better *your* life, to better *your* position in life." Participants in the study were reluctant to recognize anything more than teaching the interpersonal skills needed to "fit into" society and encouraging respect for others as service to the community. When asked specifically about additional mandates, like building a competitive workforce, people reasoned that

---

[35] Ibid., p. 14.

such goals were best reached by concentrating on individuals; if every child received a sound education, society would reap the benefits.[36]

Although Americans have always placed a premium on educating individuals, the corollary social and political mandates, like completing the great work of the American Revolution, appear to have moved to the back of people's minds. When researchers asked people whether they could think of a broader public mission for the schools in 1995, they had difficulty even understanding the question.

The 1995 research was focused exclusively on schools, yet I suspect the questions raised then would get much the same response today. But what if people were asked about the future of their community instead? Would they make a connection to schools? The answer seems to be "yes"—if something happens to provoke this insight.[37]

In his study of "Mansfield" (the fictional name of a real town in the rural Midwest), Alan Peshkin identified one provocation: a crisis. When Peshkin first asked residents what they wanted their school to do for the community, he got the same response Kettering researchers did. People appeared to have nothing in mind other than helping individual children master basic academic subjects so they could get good jobs or go on to college. Residents of Mansfield didn't even talk about their school as a resource for developing skills needed to bolster the town's sagging economy.[38]

That all changed when the county proposed closing Mansfield's school and building a consolidated one for the area. Despite arguments that the consolidated school would offer a richer curriculum and be less costly to taxpayers, people rose up in arms over the proposal. When Mansfielders thought about the purpose of schooling, Peshkin found that they talked about what was best for their children—and acceptable for their community. When they turned their attention to the threat of consolidation, they talked about what was best for the community—and acceptable for their children.[39]

---

[36] The Harwood Group, *Halfway out the Door*, pp. 8-10.

[37] In addition to reports cited earlier, see The Harwood Institute, *The Public Learning Journey: What It Takes, How to Make It* (Dayton, OH: Report to the Kettering Foundation, 2002), p. 12.

[38] Alan Peshkin, *Growing Up American: Schooling and the Survival of Community* (Chicago: University of Chicago Press, 1978), pp. 3-4, 200-202, 239.

[39] Ibid., pp. 53-55, 202.

When Mansfield faced the prospect of losing its school, townspeople suddenly had no trouble identifying the role the school played in maintaining their community. The school fostered the things most people valued: an intimate sense of belonging and a nurturing environment, which made for a particular way of life. The school reinforced the social norms that sustained this way of life—respect, responsibility, reciprocity. Had Peshkin used the concepts that became popular in the 1990s, he might have said that the school "funded" the community with essential social capital.

Some towns like Mansfield may save their schools when faced with similar threats. Most will not if they wait until there is a crisis before recognizing the community-maintaining role of schools. In Chapter 6, I'll suggest one way the interrelationship of schools and community might be kept visible.

To be clear: I am not proposing a community focus as an alternative to an individual/academic focus. Recognizing that schools are essential to creating the kind of community people want doesn't trump the importance of their role in educating children. To the contrary, the two purposes complement one another.

The way schools and communities are intertwined was captured in a report done for the Federal Writers' Project during the Great Depression. Rachel Evans told a reporter for the project that her community, a poor, coal-mining area, was "hell bent" on supporting its school. She was emphatic: "I don't see how we'd get along without our school." It was, she explained, critical to the very sense of community: "We'd never get together in a bunch if it weren't for the P.T.A. and school meetin's. You've just got to have somethin' to work together on if you ever feel at home in a place."[40]

Evans felt so strongly about the school's role in the community that she was determined to speak out—even though soon she wouldn't have a single child enrolled. "I won't stop fightin' for the others," she vowed. "I promised if they stuck by me, I'd stick by them." Her determination came from her appreciation for the instruction her children had received when they had been in the school, particularly Joanie, who had "a head full of good sense,"

---

[40] Nettie S. McDonald, "I'm Crazy 'Bout Rats," in *Up before Daylight: Life Histories from the Alabama Writers' Project, 1938-1939*, ed. James Seay Brown Jr. (Tuscaloosa: University of Alabama Press, 1982), p. 85.

and Faye, her "smartest," who was "double-promoted twice" and seemed destined to fulfill Rachel's dream for her own life—becoming a school teacher.[41] Aware of the dual role of the school in creating a sense of community and educating children, Rachel Evans wasn't about to stand on the sidelines.

Bureaucratic Barriers

Schools and communities are natural allies, and yet they can be estranged. Arguably, some tension is inevitable and perhaps helpful. After all, professional educators are supposed to have knowledge that is not generally available, and that occasionally puts them at odds with what passes as conventional wisdom. That said, the differences between educators and citizens usually come from other sources.

One of the principal forces pushing citizens to the sidelines is the bureaucratic nature of many school systems. It is all too easy to blame bureaucrats, and I don't intend to do that. There are reasons—good reasons—for the bureaucratic character of systems, even though a bureaucracy causes problems for citizens, communities, and even professional educators. School administrators are not insensitive automatons. But they have to work within bureaucratic structures and reflect the values that bureaucracies promote: efficiency, uniformity, and accountability. Bureaucracies protect schools from "arbitrary and capricious interventions," and they keep institutions within legal guidelines. These very strengths, however, tend to make bureaucracies inflexible and unresponsive to external direction. For example, the complexity, degree of detail, and number of school policies make them less accessible to the unorganized citizenry than to the organized. Bureaucracies in education also "lessen the ability of schools to adapt and change."[42]

Large bureaucracies are inherently impersonal; administrators can't deal with everyone directly. In addition, bureaucracies have to divide into subunits to administer all of their programs. The result is that when people try to find the right person to see, they are often told, "it's not my department." This is one way that school systems lose the

---

[41] Ibid., pp. 83-85.

[42] David T. Conley, *Roadmap to Restructuring: Policies, Practices, and the Emerging Visions of Schooling* (Eugene: ERIC Clearinghouse on Educational Management, University of Oregon, 1993), p. 311.

character of local agencies and become walled off from the community as quasigovernmental institutions.[43]

The school Rachel Evans' children attended was not bureaucratic. Though lacking in resources, the school was the community in another form; it was familiar, organic, and authentic. Bureaucracies seldom have any of these qualities, although they can be helpful. They may be important to a community, but they aren't a product of its efforts. While listed in the telephone directory, they aren't embedded in the local civic infrastructure. And they aren't always linked to the social, economic, and political networks that are a community's circulatory system.

School bureaucracies have ballooned with programs and mandates coming from all sides: local, state, and federal agencies. New programs have required new staff; by the 1960s, the school district in New York City had more public administrators than France. Every program had its own set of rules. In California, 200 pages of regulations in 1900 grew to 2,600 in 1985. The increase in size, however, hasn't been as significant as what this growth has done to make bureaucracies even more bureaucratic.[44]

Schools and government bureaucracies both face persistent questions about their legitimacy and accountability. And as they try to demonstrate their accountability, they are trapped in a cruel Catch-22 that undermines what are often sincere efforts to be more responsive. Brian Cook, who studies public administration, has observed that "an increasingly vicious circle has emerged in which anxiety about control and accountability . . . has led to more extensive, more complex controls, which in turn have increased the bureaucratic distance between administrators and the public they are expected to serve. This distance then raises new worries about control and accountability and brings about the introduction of another layer of controls." Cook goes on to argue that the result has been the opposite of what

---

[43] The people interviewed for the Mid-continent Research for Education and Learning study often cited bureaucratic rules and policies as a major source of their dissatisfaction with schools. Goodwin and Arens, *No Community Left Behind?*, p. 37.

[44] See David Tyack and Larry Cuban, *Tinkering toward Utopia: A Century of Public School Reform* (Cambridge, MA: Harvard University Press, 1995), pp. 19, 77-79, for a description of the growth in school bureaucracies.

the accountability reforms intended, which is greater effectiveness in serving the public.[45]

———————— ❖ ————————

Here is where we are at the end of Part One: Americans don't think they should be on the sidelines in matters of education, yet the forces that put them there will be difficult for both citizens and educators to overcome. Past school reforms that gave lip service to public participation have left what researchers describe as a legacy of distrust. The ever-increasing bureaucratization of schools has resulted in ever-increasing frustration for both teachers and citizens. Defensive, hands-off professionalism (claiming that the classroom is like an operating room) alienates would-be allies in the community. On the public side of the divide, the prospect of a consumer-like constituency for the public schools is troubling.

There are potential counterforces to these trends, but they have to be marshaled. Increasing the amount of public work done in education, for instance, would be helpful, although the kind of work citizens can do today has to be different from what they did a century ago. More recognition of the community-maintaining role of public schools could also make a difference, yet that won't happen without a well-designed strategy, which has to make sense to civic groups and to educators. Cities and towns that depend on the community-maintaining work of schools have reason to "own" and support them, but what would educators gain? From a purely professional point of view, the answer could be "nothing," assuming everything that affects the academic achievement of children happens inside the classroom. But it doesn't. There are resources outside the schools that could be put to more effective use in combating negative influences that constantly interfere with learning. Even so, neither professionals nor citizens are exactly sure of what the public can do to make a significant difference in the education of young people.[46] The next section doesn't answer these questions, but it tries to point in directions where answers might be found.

---

[45] Brian J. Cook, *Bureaucracy and Self-Government: Reconsidering the Role of Public Administration in American Politics* (Baltimore: Johns Hopkins University Press, 1996), pp. 134-135.

[46] Mary Olson and Naomi Cottoms, *The State of School-Community Relations: Rage and Blame*, report 2, part 1, *Academic Distress: A Community Issue* (Dayton, OH: Report to the Kettering Foundation, February 2001), pp. 1-4.

PART TWO:
RETHINKING
"THE PUBLIC"

WHAT ONLY THE PUBLIC CAN DO

PUBLIC BUILDING

PRACTICES THAT EMPOWER

CHAPTER FOUR
WHAT ONLY THE PUBLIC CAN DO

Pointing out that forces like bureaucratization push the schools away from the public doesn't make the case that the public *should be* rejoined with the schools or that public ownership can contribute to the instruction of young people. The claim that the public must own the schools is based, in part, on the conviction that ownership is implicit in self-rule. I have sketched out that argument in the discussion of democracy in the Introduction. The claim that public ownership is crucial is also based on the assumption that public work, which comes from ownership, makes unique and invaluable contributions to schooling and education.

The Opportunities

When Americans have thought long and hard about how to get the kind of education they want for children, some have decided that linking the schools to the community could both improve education and also "simultaneously chip away at, or even break down, the invisible barriers that have grown up and walled the schools off from those they serve." People also recognize that classroom material becomes more meaningful to students if they see its applications in everyday life. And in certain communities, citizens have seen how local educational resources can be used to reinforce their schools.[1]

The public could certainly help combat the negative forces that invade classrooms from the outside. Even professional educators who doubt that citizens have much to offer the schools (except financial support) realize that communities harbor negative influences that interfere with learning. These outside influences have been at work for so long before youngsters arrive in classrooms that schools alone can't possibly offset their "trajectories," James Traub argued in the *New York Times Magazine*.[2]

---

[1] Doble Research Associates, *Education and the Public: Summaries of Five Research Projects* (Dayton, OH: Report to the Kettering Foundation, March 1996), p. 5.

[2] James Traub, "What No School Can Do," *New York Times Magazine* (January 16, 2000): 52.

In 2004, Richard Rothstein assembled extensive research demonstrating the influence that parents' occupations, social class, community culture, and health (among other factors) have on the academic performance of children. As evidence of the power of these influences, Rothstein showed that academic gains made during the school year are often wiped out during the summer vacation months, when outside forces are at play. Although these external influences do not touch every family, they do result in differences in what happens in upper- and middle-class households as compared to lower-class households. Rothstein concluded that, "no matter how competent the teacher, the academic achievement of lower-class children will, on average, almost inevitably be less than that of middle-class children."[3]

Why these disparities? Differences in the circumstances of lower-class children stand out. They have poorer vision on average. They also have fewer books in their homes. Culture and social class are factors. For example, class and work experiences affect the way parents read to their children. When working-class parents read aloud, studies show that they tend to tell children not to interrupt. If they ask their children questions about a book, they usually ask about facts. Middle-class parents, on the other hand, are more likely to ask questions that call for interpreting the text.[4]

Clarence Stone's research has also shown that "schools cannot do it alone" because of the influence of the socioeconomic background of students. And Robert Putnam reached a similar conclusion; in fact, he has argued that "the most powerful correlate of educational outcomes is social capital at the community level."[5] The research is clear: School

---

[3] Richard Rothstein, *Class and Schools: Using Social, Economic, and Educational Reform to Close the Black-White Achievement Gap* (Washington, DC: Economic Policy Institute, 2004), p. 2.

[4] Ibid., pp. 2-3, 20-21, 57.

[5] Clarence N. Stone, "Linking Civic Capacity and Human Capital Formation," in *Strategies for School Equity: Creating Productive Schools in a Just Society*, ed. Marilyn J. Gittell (New Haven: Yale University Press, 1998), p. 163 and Robert D. Putnam, "Community-Based Social Capital and Educational Performance," in *Making Good Citizens: Education and Civil Society*, ed. Diane Ravitch and Joseph P. Viteritti (New Haven: Yale University Press, 2001), pp. 72 (the quote here refers to elementary school test scores) and 81-82. For more on out-of-school influences, see James P. Comer, *Waiting for a Miracle: Why Schools Can't Solve Our Problems—And How We Can* (New York: Dutton, 1997).

performance is materially affected by community mobilization, civic capacity, and social capital. And the public can do something about all of these.

Creating Places for Learning

The public's role becomes more apparent when the focus is on all that affects learning rather than on schooling alone. As discussed earlier, Americans have created a host of educating institutions other than schools (lyceums, museums, libraries). And they have used the culture itself to educate through festivals, patriotic celebrations, and political rallies. Parents, in particular, have had definite responsibilities for moral education and even certain kinds of instruction, such as reading, which was once a prerequisite for entering school. Families were supported by educational institutions like Sunday schools, which were first organized to provide elementary instruction.[6]

Asked to describe where education occurs today, people continue to list more than schools. They talk about churches, field trips, television, zoos, youth organizations and, most of all, the workplace. What young people learn from these educating institutions is much like what they learn in schools: skills and values, history and foreign languages, and other cultures.[7] These institutions demonstrate that *the community itself is an educational institution.* A community owes its citizens more than safe streets, clean water, and fire protection. Every community owes its citizens opportunities to educate themselves.[8]

---

[6] Lawrence Cremin has shown that education is more than schooling in his multivolume series *American Education.* He listed "families, churches, libraries, museums, publishers, benevolent societies, youth groups, agricultural fairs, radio networks, military organizations, and research institutions." He also included newspapers and television. Cremin criticized historians like Ellwood P. Cubberly for not pointing out that it takes more than just an understanding of schools to understand American education. Lawrence A. Cremin, *American Education: The Colonial Experience, 1607-1783* (New York: Harper and Row, 1970), p. xi. Also see Cremin's books *The Wonderful World of Ellwood Patterson Cubberly* (New York: Bureau of Publications, Teachers College, Columbia University, 1965); *American Education: The National Experience, 1783-1876* (New York: Harper and Row, 1980); and *American Education: The Metropolitan Experience, 1876-1980* (New York: Harper and Row, 1988).

[7] Doble Research Associates, *Summaries of Five Research Projects* (Dayton, OH: Report to the Kettering Foundation, 1995), p. 4.

[8] The ideal that a community owes "its members the fullest opportunity for development" is as powerful as it is novel. I appreciate Margaret Holt, a Kettering associate, for bringing it to my attention. This quotation is from an article John Dewey wrote on "The School as Social Center," *Elementary School Teacher* 3 (October 1902): 86.

I mentioned that the foundation has been particularly struck not only by the difference in the meanings of "schools" and "education" but also by the emotions associated with the words. School reminds people of things that have a negative connotation like violence and bureaucracy. Education, on the other hand, is associated with "knowledge, opportunity and experience"—all positive.[9] One reason for the different reactions may be that people believe that even though they can't "school," they can educate.

This distinction was quite obvious in Baton Rouge, Louisiana, when a group of 12 randomly selected people were asked whether they had ever had experience educating someone. Diverse as their experiences had been, no one had any difficulty giving example after example of direct and meaningful ways in which they had taught—through literacy programs, jobs, churches, and a variety of community projects.[10] People not only taught some of the same subjects covered in schools, but also taught "the value of education through the medium of hard work." This particular "lesson" can transfer to the classroom and has a significant effect on young people, according to a study of immigrant and migrant families whose children were "highly successful in school."[11]

People who have been involved in some type of education (broadly defined) have done so for a variety of social, political, and economic reasons: to eliminate racism, strengthen the economy, and safeguard the environment, to mention a few. In fact, some type of education is considered necessary to secure nearly everything people value in their communities: safety, tolerance, caring, fairness. When people acknowledge that "education is important to everything," they reason that "education is everyone's responsibility." That is why putting the burden of solving the problems of education solely on the schools doesn't make sense. The traditional faith in education as a

---

[9] Doble Research Associates, *Summaries of Five Research Projects*, p. 3.

[10] John Doble to the Kettering Foundation's Comprehensive Educational Resources Project Work Group, memorandum, "Project Update," April 13, 1992, p. 3.

[11] The study was done by Gerardo López in 2001 and cited in Anne T. Henderson and Karen L. Mapp, *A New Wave of Evidence: The Impact of School, Family, and Community Connections on Student Achievement* (Austin, TX: Southwest Educational Development Laboratory, 2002), pp. 49, 138-139.

means of reform isn't dead, but it is a faith in education writ large, not just in schooling.

Americans may start out conflating education with schooling until someone points out that education does not occur just in the classroom. That recognition turns conversations in a different direction; the focus moves from schools to community. "We need to talk about education and our community together," some people have said, "so that we can see what we really want out of education."[12]

Harnessing All That Educates

Once citizens think about the role the community might play, they don't have problems identifying institutions other than schools that educate. Several years ago, a citizens' group in Chattanooga, Tennessee, drew a map showing where their educating institutions were located; they were everywhere. Businesses, for instance, taught in much the way craft guilds did centuries ago, through the apprentice system. Each institution brought its own unique resources to bear on education. The resources in Chattanooga are available in almost every city. A zoo can use real animals to teach biology; a storage company can teach about space; a carpenter can teach elementary math with rulers and boards.[13]

Doble Research found people who were quite convinced that the education "out there" could enrich the instruction that goes on in schools. "What they're teaching kids nowadays in classrooms is not what they will need to survive in this world" was a frequent observation, which led to suggestions like "show them what the company does," or "kids should get exposure to the jobs they might be doing."[14]

The conviction that the "education out there" can be put to good use has stimulated interest in projects that resonate with Howard Gardner's research showing that there are different types of human intelligence. Because there is more than one kind of intelligence, it follows that there has to be more than one way to learn. For instance, Gardner thinks that educating institutions other than schools are

[12] Doble Research Associates, *The Comprehensive Educational Resources Inventory: An Analytic Summary of the Results from the CERI Research* (Dayton, OH: Report to the Kettering Foundation, 1994), pp. 3-5.

[13] Kathleen Martin, telephone interview by Gina Paget, transcript, June 22, 1995, Kettering Foundation, Dayton, OH.

[14] Doble Research Associates, *Summaries of Five Research Projects*, pp. 3-5.

best for "hands-on, minds-on" instruction. Not a fan of occasional site visits, he advocates regular, integrated experiences with community institutions.[15]

Gardner's advice has found a following in place-based instruction. For example, PACERS, a cooperative association of rural schools in Alabama, has used solar homes, greenhouses, fishponds, and newsrooms as learning laboratories. In Florala, Alabama, a teacher, John Harbuck, used an aquaculture facility built by the community to make science relevant. Florala is a short drive from the Gulf of Mexico, where fishing is a way of life, so schoolchildren know that fish are important. They were eager to learn about pH levels and water chemistry because, as one youngster put it, they didn't want the fish to go "belly-up." The community not only furnished the teaching facility but also provided knowledge of the Gulf.[16]

If citizens work with citizens (including teachers and principals) to build a fishpond for teaching science, they have a better chance of bringing about enduring improvements. Why? As educational reformers have pointed out, trying to change what happens in schools without using a democratic process of change is merely "technocracy" and will not last.[17] When the community at large is involved in creating facilities like the PACERS' learning laboratories and the schools are receptive to outside assistance, the public's sense of ownership should also grow.

The claim being made here—that the community can educate—is easier to accept if the community is middle class. The claim is more controversial if the community is in a poor, urban neighborhood or rural area. Poor people are thought to be too busy surviving to worry about civic matters. Even if they do worry, conventional wisdom says, they don't have the political power or resources to accomplish anything.

---

[15] Howard E. Gardner's research is reported in *The Unschooled Mind: How Children Think and How Schools Should Teach* (New York: Basic Books, 1991).

[16] Jack Shelton, *Consequential Learning: A Public Approach to Better Schools* (Montgomery, AL: NewSouth Books, 2005), pp. 69-70, 100-109. Shelton, who directed PACERS out of The University of Alabama's Program for Rural Services and Research, documented the impact of community laboratories on classroom performance.

[17] Mario Fantini, Marilyn Gittell, and Richard Magat, *Community Control and the Urban School* (New York: Praeger Publishers, 1970), p. 175.

Certainly, poor communities lack the resources available elsewhere. In fact, few communities are entirely self-sufficient. Most have to depend on other communities for particular kinds of resources, often financial capital. That doesn't mean, however, that people in impoverished areas are without any capabilities. A study done by the Hubert H. Humphrey Institute at the University of Minnesota found that poor people with little formal schooling have a range of skills and experiences to share with youngsters.[18] Other case studies from low-income neighborhoods across the country support the Humphrey Institute's findings.

A good example is a project involving several inner-city churches.[19] Participants in a church workshop responded to a series of questions: What do you know how to do well? Where did you learn it? What helped you learn it? Have you ever taught anyone anything? What do you think made your teaching effective?[20] People's first reaction was, "I never taught anybody anything," perhaps because they associated teaching with classrooms. Later, however, they described numerous ways in which they had, in fact, educated others. They had taught basic reading and mathematics as well as skills like cooking, sewing, and taking care of equipment. Their "lessons" included the virtues of patience, persistence, and sacrifice.

Sometimes, participants in the church workshops felt hopeless and thought of themselves as victims with little power. Still, they appreciated the value of education, which one participant called "the best thing in the world." And that prompted them to become civic actors. For example, a group of African American church members were worried that young people in their neighborhood had little opportunity to learn anything useful. So they decided to expose their

---

[18] Project Public Life, *Teaching Politics: A Report from the Third Annual Project Public Life Working Conference* (Minneapolis: Project Public Life, Humphrey Institute of Public Affairs, 1991). Also see *The Solomon Project Annual Report* (Minneapolis: Project Public Life, Hubert Humphrey Institute of Public Affairs, 1992).

[19] The results of the project carried out from 1992 to 1994 were reported in Doble Research Associates, *Take Charge Workshop Series: Description and Findings from the Field* (Dayton, OH: Report to the Kettering Foundation, 1994).

[20] These questions came out of the Solomon Project, which worked with low-income communities in Minneapolis to "recognize their own educational capacities." See *The Solomon Project Annual Report.*

youngsters to something new and interesting at least once a month. They took charge of their children's education.[21]

Using Public Work

Cases like these suggest that America could increase its capacity to educate many times over if it harnessed all its educational resources. Citizens have any number of ways to be the authors of the education they would like young people to have.[22] The learning resources that are made available through the collective efforts of citizens are doubly important because the work involved in creating the resources also builds the public—the kind of public that schools and communities need. I don't mean to slight the valuable partnerships schools have formed with businesses and other institutions, but they can't substitute for the partnerships with a citizenry-at-work.

People taking charge of education, everyone with a part to play —it sounds great. Why isn't this happening everywhere? Former National Education Association President Mary Hatwood Futrell may have put her finger on the reason when she observed that, although many proposals have called for more school-community collaboration, "the question of who should do what is left unanswered." In what I have written so far, I have already sketched out a general answer to that question, but I'll give some more examples of activities that help define the roles citizens can play, both educational and political.

Public Work to Reinforce Schools

The connection between the work citizens do and the ability of young people to succeed academically is often hard to make, so I'll start with what the public can do to support classroom instruction.

Enlisting Everyone in Teaching the Kids: When people become directly involved in teaching through churches, youth organizations, libraries, and museums, their participation sends a message that education is everyone's responsibility. It creates a social norm, which has been evident in comments like, "Everybody is trying to teach the kids." That was said in Atlanta following a concerted effort in the 1980s to involve the entire community. Businesses began to sponsor

---

[21] Doble Research Associates, *Take Charge Workshop Series*, p. 5.

[22] I got this idea from Lawrence Cremin, whose prize-winning history of American education gave me an appreciation for all that educates.

magnet schools, while churches and synagogues ran tutorial programs. The city was attempting to teach its young people by using all its educational resources.[23] Communities that consciously try to educate as communities educate best. They provide the social reinforcement that students need.

In Tennessee, Governor Lamar Alexander mounted a vigorous community-based campaign to improve schools. As he had hoped, test scores improved—but before legislated reforms were implemented.[24] How could that have happened? The governor insisted that "communities fix schools" and that apparently started people thinking about what they should do, rather than depend entirely on the state. Alexander's community-by-community strategy preceding the legislation sent a powerful message: People thought what teachers did was important, and they cared whether or not students learned. Because learning is affected by community expectations, the improvement in test scores shouldn't have been surprising.[25]

Outside Tennessee, communities have done what Governor Alexander encouraged by turning school reform efforts into community-based educational projects. In Arkansas, Helena was stunned when the state placed its school district in "Phase I of Academic Distress" because more than half of the students scored in the bottom quartile on standardized tests. Citizens were angry and looked for someone to blame; teachers and school administrators were the prime suspects. Finally,

---

[23] Alonzo A. Crim, "A Community of Believers Creates a Community of Achievers," *Educational Record* 68/69 (Fall 1987/Winter 1988): 45.

[24] Jennie Vanetta Carter Thomas, "How Three Governors Involved the Public in Passing Their Education Reform Programs" (EdD diss., George Peabody College for Teachers of Vanderbilt University, 1992), pp. 35-36.

[25] James S. Coleman and Thomas Hoffer found that the motivating power of individual adults who were connected socially and able to establish common expectations regarding the behavior of young people is especially influential. See Coleman and Hoffer, *Public and Private High Schools: The Impact of Communities* (New York: Basic Books, 1987), pp. 221-233.

Governor Alexander's slogan "Communities Fix Schools" has been the theme of other successful efforts to use community-based strategies to improve student achievement. The work of 19 community-organizing groups is described in a study by Eva Gold, Elaine Simon, and Chris Brown, *Successful Community Organizing for School Reform* (Chicago: Cross City Campaign for Urban School Reform, March 2002).

people began asking, what is the real issue here? Working with a civic organization, Walnut Street Works, they took the problem to a series of town meetings. As people struggled with what should be done, it became clear that the schools weren't the only institutions that were responsible. As a result of shifting the focus to the entire community, citizens decided to enlist all of their educating institutions in getting at the problems that endangered the schools.[26]

Providing a Real-World Context for Learning: Familiar settings and routines provide a context that encourages students to learn. Grocery stores, restaurants, even subways help make abstract academic subjects relevant. Context gives learning purpose and meaning. In Jackson County, Kentucky, for example, where quilting is a familiar activity, the K-3 Mathematics Project used quilts to teach basic geometric concepts. Cutting shapes out of construction paper to make patterns for quilt patches made the concepts of triangle and pentangle concrete, understandable, and significant.[27]

Citizens appreciate the importance of showing youngsters that what may seem purely academic subjects have practical uses. At a town meeting in Baton Rouge, one woman explained:

> I believe that schools should be teaching math and that [students] should go to these places [in the community] to practice the concepts you learn in school or to see how they are applied. In a library, you practice the skills you learned about research and referencing, in a museum you see a mummy which you learned about in school. Kids should go to Exxon and see on-the-job application of the trigonometry they've learned.[28]

The most familiar and often-cited case demonstrating the power of community context comes from the work of Robert Moses, a civil rights activist in Mississippi during the 1960s and a recipient of a

---

[26] Mary Olson and Naomi Cottoms, *The State of School-Community Relations: Rage and Blame*, report 2, part 1, *Academic Distress: A Community Issue* (Dayton, OH: Report to the Kettering Foundation, February 2001).

[27] Susan Ohanian, *Garbage Pizza, Patchwork Quilts, and Math Magic: Stories about Teachers Who Love to Teach and Children Who Love to Learn* (New York: W. H. Freeman, 1992), pp. 184-187.

[28] John Doble to Damon Higgins and Randa Slim, memorandum, "Report on *CERI* Community Leadership Workshop Baton Rouge, LA, 6/23/93," July 19, 1993, p. 4.

MacArthur Foundation "genius" grant. Moses captured the Baton Rouge woman's vision in his Algebra Project in a Massachusetts school. Believing that difficult mathematical concepts could be more readily explained to students if the concepts were linked to everyday applications, he found that he could use the familiar Red Line subway route from Cambridge to Boston to explain negative numbers. Before Moses introduced this project, few students in the school took the advanced-placement qualifying exam in mathematics, and only a few of those who did passed. After ten years with the program in place, the school's graduates ranked second in the city's advanced-placement test scores.[29]

In other communities, citizens have found contexts for learning in equally ordinary places. In Dayton, Ohio, business owners and educators have used restaurants as language labs. El Meson, which features South American food, has served lunch to schoolchildren in a setting where only Spanish is spoken. The entire staff of the restaurant is involved in public work. At Mamma DiSalvo's family restaurant across town, linguini has accompanied linguistics in Italian classes. Rather than volunteering to help inside the schools, the people involved in projects like these are complementing what happens in classrooms with experiences that can be had only outside them.

Making Substantive Knowledge Available: Schools are known as repositories of substantive knowledge: mathematics, history, literature. Communities, on the other hand, aren't assumed to have that kind of knowledge—only practical tips on how to get along in the world. That assumption just isn't valid. Other community institutions can't replace the schools, yet many of them teach the same subjects taught in classrooms. Two obvious examples: natural history museums offer courses in ecology, and art museums teach art history.

The potential for school-community collaboration in academic fields is enormous. A study in seven cities across the country found a broad spectrum of community organizations teaching subjects that might supplement school curricula. The list of organizations included eight science museums, four history museums, two art museums, seven theaters, one choir, one orchestra, and four libraries. Thirteen other institutions—for example, the Latin American Family Day

---

[29] Alexis Jetter, "Mississippi Learning," *New York Times*, February 21, 1993.

Center in Charlotte, North Carolina; the YMCA in Willimantic, Connecticut; the North Carolina Zoological Park; and the Trailside Nature Center in Cincinnati, Ohio—also reported offering substantive classes. In just 7 cities, more than 40 teaching organizations were identified with courses ranging from the Ice Age to Egyptian Textiles to the Planetary System.[30]

Courses taught outside the classroom have characteristics that make them ideal for complementing academic instruction. Lauren Resnick's research has shown that schools focus primarily on individual learners, while other community institutions teach youngsters to learn together as part of working together. Her studies also found that schools tend to encourage symbolic and abstract thinking, while instruction outside the school is more likely to be concrete and practical.[31]

Offsetting Negative Influences: I have already presented research showing that economic, cultural, and other influences outside the schools push students onto paths that professional educators have difficulty changing despite their best efforts. Even with the help of supportive parents, teachers can't do all we expect of them—and that many expect of themselves. What can citizens do to help?

No community can erase poverty or eliminate class differences, but every community can improve the environment in which schools operate. Even modest changes count. Kansas City's Local INvestment Commission (LINC) helped citizens organize an escort service in their neighborhoods to protect children walking to and from schools. The service didn't work miracles in the classroom. It certainly didn't eliminate the crime that had overrun low-income neighborhoods. Yet the escorts did increase safety on the streets and got students to school

---

[30] Kathy Whyde Jesse to David Mathews et al., memorandum, "Newspaper Study," April 18, 1994. Also see Anne T. Henderson and Karen L. Mapp, *A New Wave of Evidence: The Impact of School, Family, and Community Connections on Student Achievement* (Austin, TX: Southwest Educational Development Laboratory, 2002), pp. 8, 68. The report of this laboratory was filled with "examples of collaboration between school leaders and community groups that have contributed to improved facilities, more funding resources, higher-quality academic programs, improved social and health services, and new after-school programs."

[31] Lauren B. Resnick, "Learning In School and Out," *Educational Researcher* 16 (December 1987): 13-20.

without incident. More important, adults walking with children provided a valuable civic lesson in responsibility.[32]

Public Work in the Politics of Education

Everyone agrees that citizens play a critical political role in supporting schools: voting on school bond issues and tax levies, electing board members, running for a board position. But is that all? I don't think so. As I've said before, the public's most basic political role is to decide where a democratic society should be headed—to decide on its ultimate purposes. The citizenry is not just a means to ends that have already been determined elsewhere in the political system. Though not intentional, that is the implication when the public is treated as a supporting cast for schools. Who should decide what is in the best interest of the citizenry as a whole? Difficult as that is, only the public can do it—the public that forms in the process of making collective decisions.

Establishing Mandates: Chapter 2 described the mandates citizens gave the first schools. Schools were to help create a way of life in which social responsibility would be the norm, to encourage young people to be industrious, and to teach the subjects that an educated person was expected to master. Schools also had responsibilities to democracy itself. They were to weave a social fabric out of a variety of threads such as diverse interests, classes, and cultures. Above all, they were to raise up a new generation of citizens. The public work involved in deciding on these mandates gave the schools legitimacy.

Developing school mandates from the objectives of communities has practical advantages today. Being grounded in the common purposes of a community helps schools counter narrowly focused disputes or "solution wars." These wars go on endlessly when various factions repeat well-rehearsed proposals: Teachers press for more funds; taxpayers want to eliminate what they consider waste; business leaders insist on better management. The wars drive most citizens away, even if the various proposals have merit. The sound of conflict drowns out all else and creates the sense that "the

[32] Collaborative Communications Group, *New Relationships with Schools: Organizations That Build Community by Connecting with Schools* (Dayton, OH: Report to the Kettering Foundation, May 2003), pp. 17-19.

different factions in this community no longer appear to be working for the common good . . . it's too much of 'I want this and she wants that.'"[33]

Schools that have mandates from an inclusive public have a counterbalance to requirements placed on them to serve a host of disparate interests. These requirements result in a multitude of categorical programs that serve only one particular group of students or deal with only one facet of a problem. Advocates of these programs often have a legitimate claim on the schools, and categorical programs usually have worthy goals. Still, educators and school trustees find themselves pulled in many and often conflicting directions. Tensions become quite severe when school districts have to provide funding. The decisions citizens make on broad mandates for schools won't exempt districts from meeting legally binding requirements, but they might give school boards a basis for adjudicating competing claims.

Adding a Public Voice: To have a mandate from a community as a whole, the citizenry must speak in a coherent voice that reflects their shared judgment about the kind of community they want to be. Without that voice, schools are helpless before the besieging forces of individual interests. But how is such a public voice created?

A community can't speak in a public voice or know what James Madison called its "permanent and enduring interest" until people have struggled seriously, much as a good jury does, with the tough decisions that are always required on major issues. Unless that work is done, there isn't a public voice to hear. We can describe our own particular concerns, but that doesn't tell us whether our concerns are shared or how our interests may be interrelated. And asking me what I think or want doesn't reveal what we think or want. We can't know what we think until we have listened to one another and grappled together with difficult choices. We aren't really thinking as a public until that happens.

A genuine public voice emerges when three conditions have been met. First, a diverse body of citizens has to talk, preferably face-to-face (as opposed to sitting in an audience and being talked to). Second, the framework for the conversations has to present all the

---

[33] The Harwood Group, *Hard Talk Discussion Group Report: Insights into How Citizens Talk about Education and Community* (Dayton, OH: Report to the Kettering Foundation, 1991), pp. 1, 14-15.

major options for action fairly, each with both its advantages and disadvantages disclosed. Finally, people have to weigh the costs and benefits of each option until they get a sense of what the community will and won't do to address the problem at hand.

There are communities where these conditions have been met—or met enough to produce a public voice. In the Philadelphia area, school districts used public forums to help form a public voice that balanced what would otherwise have been only the voices of special interests. The forums were sponsored in partnership with civic organizations, the public library, and the local newspaper.[34]

When I say that the public voice reflects shared concerns, I am not saying it is a single, homogeneous voice. It couldn't be, because the public in our democracy is not a homogeneous body. Neither is the voice one of consensus. For example, members of the citizen groups that responded to desegregation orders in the 1970s had conflicting views. Some favored complete and immediate integration of the schools; others, who opposed integration, were concerned with preventing racial strife. With considerable difficulty, some of these groups were eventually able to speak in a coherent voice that helped their communities find practical solutions to emotionally charged issues. Committee members never agreed on much, but they were able to describe their problem in a way that captured the major concerns of a diverse citizenry. And that made the interrelation of different interests more apparent. Integration wasn't going to proceed as it should without engaging at least some of the opposition, and community stability wasn't likely to be maintained without the participation of those who insisted that segregation end immediately. A public voice is distinctive in that it is inclusive and yet coherent; it reflects a synthesis of individual views as they both diverge and converge.

⁑

I have tried to make the case that there is essential work in education that only citizens can do—without giving the impression that the public is merely a source of support for the schools. As I've said before, people know that they aren't a means to the ends of educators. Those who aren't parents, in particular, may want to know whether the

[34] Harris Sokoloff, "A Deliberative Model for Engaging the Community: Use of Community Forums Can Undercut Special-Interest Politics," *School Administrator* 53 (November 1996): 12-18.

schools are "with them" and their problems before they are willing to discuss whether they are "with the schools." While this chapter has been about what the public does, the next one deals with a prior issue —how the public comes to be.

CHAPTER FIVE
PUBLIC
BUILDING

If the public has invaluable contributions to make to education, as the last chapter argues, then we need to know as much as we can about how a public forms or about the process of public building.[1] I believe answers can come from looking at how Americans go about collective work—at what they do and not just who they are.

In the Beginning . . .

Public work is the culmination of a long process, and the formative stages are critical. I stress these stages because they prepare people for public work the way reading readiness prepares people to read. Richard Harwood has charted this progression, and I have incorporated his analysis into this chapter, along with findings from Kettering research. While Harwood could distinguish one step or stage from another, he was impressed by how they flow together. He discovered that the "flow" or slow movement toward political participation is more important than any single step.[2]

Early on, participation may not seem political at all. On any given day, some people take the first step to becoming involved in community matters by talking to family and friends about something that bothers them. Then they try to find out whether anyone outside

---

[1] For a more detailed discussion of the process of forming publics, see *For Communities to Work* (Dayton, OH: Kettering Foundation, 2002).

[2] Richard Harwood is president of The Harwood Institute for Public Innovation. He has meticulously traced the way people become involved in public life in two studies: *The Engagement Path: The Realities of How People Engage over Time —And the Possibilities for Re-engaging Americans* (Washington, DC: Harwood Institute, October 2003), and an earlier report by The Harwood Group, *Meaningful Chaos: How People Form Relationships with Public Concerns* (Dayton, OH: Report to the Kettering Foundation, 1993).

this close circle is also worried. For example, a woman might talk with her neighbors about drug paraphernalia she saw in the street.[3] It may be a short conversation, probably over her backyard fence. At the next stage, conversations like this one become more structured when they are carried into churches and civic groups. Later still, town meetings might be held on what should be done to keep drugs out of the community, and people could decide on a strategy. Some of the things they decide might be carried out by ad hoc groups or civic organizations. Government agencies would probably be asked to play a role. If these sorts of problem-solving initiatives result in public work being done on problems, then a public begins to form in the community, a citizenry with the capacity for continued collective decision making and action.

Step-by-Step

Public work, like any work, requires considerable energy, which like the work itself builds in stages. Knowing what generates the energy that drives public work is important because it's easy to shut down the generators without realizing it.

Political participation begins on a very personal level. Americans worry about *their* jobs, *their* health, *their* children's education. And they keep coming back to these primary concerns, which remain political touchstones. When people are asked to consider an issue, the first thing they usually ask themselves is, does this problem affect me or my family? That question has considerable energy behind it because it calls to mind the things that touch people directly and intimately. The best public forums I have seen have started with the question, how does this problem affect you personally? Although people start with this question, it doesn't mean that they are totally selfish.

When people see a connection between a community problem and their personal interests, they are inclined to talk to other people. They are no less self-interested, but, as I said, they want to find out whether anyone else is concerned about drug paraphernalia or anything that seems threatening. People have these conversations where they normally gather. They move in and out of a great many discussions,

---

[3] A woman from Little Rock did, in fact, help develop an anticrime program, after finding syringe needles by the side of her house. The Harwood Group, *Meaningful Chaos*, pp. 11-12.

which are random and unstructured. Much of what they say may sound like small talk—with a lot of quaint stories thrown in. People are just mulling over what they hear or perhaps testing for a response: What did you see? What do you think it means? Does it worry you? At this stage, they aren't ready to make decisions; they are still checking out the situation, and that takes time. Trying to rush them along is a big mistake.

As people gather more and more information, it might seem that they would become confused, that a deluge of facts and opinions would overwhelm them. Harwood didn't find that happening. While organizations break down problems into manageable projects and professionals focus in, laserlike, on discrete phenomena, most people don't do either. They experience the combined effects of interrelated problems in their everyday lives, so they try to find out how the different pieces fit together, and their curiosity generates energy.[4] For example, when drugs are the problem, they are never the only problem. People have to consider everything from the quality of family life to the condition of the economy to the effectiveness of the police force. Citizens don't simplify issues; they try to see them in all their complexity and locate them in a web of interrelated issues.

If people realize that they share similar concerns, they feel con-nected. And making connections with other people is a potent source of political energy. The research doesn't show that people have to see the same problem in the same way, however. In fact, they seldom do because their circumstances and experiences aren't the same. If citizens realize that they all have a stake in solving a problem, albeit for different reasons, or if they sense that their interests are related, though different, they are disposed to joining forces. On the other hand, when people fail to see these interrelations or to make these connections, they tend to feel isolated and unable to make a difference. Political energy drains away.

Another source of political energy is being able to see an old problem in a new light. It helps people imagine solutions that otherwise elude them. New insights are sparked when people hear about different experiences that allow them to see familiar problems from unfamiliar vantage points. A fresh perspective reorients them and also increases their confidence that progress is possible. If people

---

[4] The Harwood Group, *Strategies for Civil Investing: Foundations and Community-Building* (Dayton, OH: Report to the Kettering Foundation, 1997), p. 8.

don't come to those insights, they remain stuck in a rut, saying the same things to the same people.

Still another burst of political energy occurs when people come to the conclusion that they themselves have to do something about their problems. This happens when citizens realize that blaming others doesn't accomplish anything, or when they get tired of waiting for someone else to rescue them. People may even discover that they are implicated in their problems—that they are accountable and have to own their problems. When they do, they are ready to take on the difficult work of deciding what to do about the things that bother them.

Although owning problems paves the way for deciding what to do about them, people don't proceed step-by-step in making decisions as they would in going up or down a staircase. They move back and forth through the earlier stages of becoming involved. They revisit the question of whether something truly valuable is at stake; they probe beneath the surface of issues for related problems; and they look for connections with others.

Public Engagement and School Engagement

What I've been describing are the evolutionary stages as citizens engage one another in public work. This type of public engagement isn't the same as the engagement that is school-centered rather than citizen-centered.

Shortly after *Is There?* was published, I was invited to a conference organized by public relations professionals in school systems and asked to talk about the new "public engagement movement." Since I had referred to an "engaged public" in the book, I accepted with the understanding that I could use half of my time to ask the conference participants how they understood "the public" and "engagement."

From what was said at the conference and from what I learned later, I got the impression that the schools' engagement movement was, in part, a response to the lack of success in urban educational reforms and a recognition that significant changes require more than strong professional leaders.[5] In this context, "engagement" meant

---

[5] This was also the conclusion of analyses reported in Jolley Bruce Christman and Amy Rhodes, *Civic Engagement and Urban School Improvement: Hard-to-Learn Lessons from Philadelphia* (Consortium for Policy Research Education, June 2002).

building a more inclusive constituency for school reform. Two-way conversations between educators and citizens werc a hallmark of the better projects. Some of these engagement campaigns set out to change school policies; others to generate more support for tax increases. Most had to do with getting communities behind their schools. That is a worthy objective, and it seems appropriate to refer to those efforts as school-centered.[6]

Amy Burke Shriberg, a researcher at Kettering, surveyed the literature on the engagement movement and found that most school-based initiatives had to do with either involving parents or developing partnerships between schools and businesses or community agencies. An Annenberg survey of engagement projects in schools reported that few of these campaigns provided opportunities for citizens to "routinely and intentionally deliberate and decide on what kind of schooling they [citizens] want for their children." Public forums might have been convened, but they were held more to inform people rather than encourage public decision making. There were exceptions, however, and the Annenberg report did cite some instances where public forums had resulted in collective decisions that led to concrete changes.[7]

Critics of the school engagement movement argue that the efforts, to this point, have not been citizen-led and haven't affected the fundamental nature of the relationship between communities and schools.[8] Perhaps the movement is still evolving and may yet shift more of its focus from school reform to the community and to public building. Several developments since *Is There?* was published suggest that such a shift may be underway. Some professionals in public relations have already recognized that engagement has to go beyond creating a better image for schools.[9] And the Southwest Educational

[6] Annenberg Institute on Public Engagement for Public Education, *Reasons for Hope, Voices for Change* (Providence, RI: Annenberg Institute for School Reform, 1998).

[7] Ibid., p. 10.

[8] Bryan Goodwin and Sheila A. Arens, *No Community Left Behind? An Analysis of the Potential Impact of the No Child Left Behind Act of 2001 on School-Community Relationships* (Dayton, OH: McREL Report to the Kettering Foundation, May 2003), pp. 7-8.

[9] National School Public Relations Association, *NSPRA/Kettering Public Engagement Project: Final Report for July 2002-December 2003* (Dayton, OH: Report to the Kettering Foundation, 2003).

Development Laboratory has reported that new initiatives by neighbor-hood-based organizations are forming around issues such as housing rather than schools. These initiatives, "markedly unlike" typical engagement efforts, are led by parents and community members and have an "overtly political" objective. Some neighborhood organiza-tions have moved on to school issues, hoping to give residents more political control over educational bureaucracies.[10]

Other community-led initiatives are neither antagonistic toward school officials nor concerned with reducing their power but rather aim to establish a different relationship with administrators. Their goal is to change "the adversarial relationships that too often exist between schools and the wider community," particularly in low-income neighborhoods.[11] After studying this type of engagement, Clarence Stone characterized it as having "less to do with challenging the control mechanisms of established elites than with the character of the conditions necessary for viable relationships." Stone found that while "adversarial methods" were used extensively in the 1960s and 1970s, their yields have proved to be "quite limited." He thinks a shift is under way to build civic capacity for problem solving.[12] Some community groups are already testing a strategy of strengthening the public's capacity to act and then using that capacity to work on problems in education.[13]

[10] Anne T. Henderson and Karen L. Mapp, *A New Wave of Evidence: The Impact of School, Family, and Community Connections on Student Achievement* (Austin, TX: Southwest Educational Development Laboratory, 2002), p. 54.

[11] Sheila Beachum Bilby, "Community School Reform: Parents Making a Difference in Education," *Mott Mosaic* 1 (December 2002): 3.

[12] Stone cited John Goodlad and others as leading the way among educators and drew examples from the Industrial Areas Foundation (IAF) and the organizing work of Ernesto Cortes. Clarence N. Stone, "The Dilemmas of Social Reform Revisited: Putting Civic Engagement in the Picture" (paper presented at the annual meeting of the American Political Science Association, Atlanta, GA, September 2-5, 1999). For more on IAF, look at Mark R. Warren, *Dry Bones Rattling: Community Building to Revitalize American Democracy* (Princeton, NJ: Princeton University Press, 2001). Also see Robert D. Putnam and Lewis M. Feldstein, *Better Together: Restoring the American Community* (New York: Simon and Schuster, 2003) for IAF and similar examples.

[13] Annenberg Institute, *Reasons for Hope, Voices for Change.* For a discussion of civic capacity building to strengthen the practices citizens use to govern themselves, consider Christman and Rhodes, *Civic Engagement and Urban School Improvement.*

I share the hope that another generation of engagement initiatives will grow from the idea that the public is more than an aggregation of individuals to be mobilized by an outside force and from the assumption that a citizenry has ways to generate its own energy. This type of engagement would lend itself to public building, which is a prerequisite to restoring public ownership of the schools, not just to generating more revenue (though I don't argue against that). In other words, I am proposing a public building type of engagement suited to democratic self-rule.

Engagement and Democracy

As discussed in the Introduction, "the people," or the public, replaced the monarchy as the sovereign power in this country. Sovereignty is defined by the strength or power to act—to decide, judge, and institute change. The power to act makes it possible to rule. It follows then that the sovereign public must do the kinds of things that monarchs once did —make decisions and act on them. This is the basis for seeing the public as more than an audience to be addressed or a market to be enticed. And it is why I have suggested that it is useful to think of a democratic citizenry as a dynamic political force. The implication of this understanding of the public is that what has to be engaged is the force itself —the force generated by a citizenry doing public work. To go back to the earlier analogy, the challenge is to plug into the electricity, not to hold onto the light bulb.

Engaging or tapping into political energy isn't the same as generating support for school reforms. If all citizens did were to consent to reforms made in their name, it would not generate much energy. "We, the People" would be no more than a persuaded populace, which isn't likely to have the power to sustain the American system of public education. While citizens may listen to reasoned arguments and collect information from others, in the end, they have to make decisions among themselves. That alone gives the people's choices moral force. Being sold on what others have decided doesn't have the same political effect—it doesn't build reservoirs of political energy. Citizens are more disposed to take ownership of what they have participated in choosing than what has been chosen for them.

This emphasis on citizens making their own decisions isn't meant to disparage the efforts of school board members and educators who have to present their plans and convince people to support them. Sometimes citizens buy what is being sold, but do they own it? Not always. People are more likely to blame the manufacturer (in this case, educators) for anything that goes wrong. Although nothing happens in a community unless someone takes the initiative, it doesn't follow that the only thing Americans have to do is sit back and wait to be convinced. Citizens are primarily responsible for engaging one another; professionals can't do that for them.

What I am saying is that engagement has to be citizen-to-citizen before it can be citizen-to-school or school-to-community. That is a tall order, I know. School folk are under considerable pressure to show immediate results from any kind of project. Yet, here is the challenge: Public engagement can't be considered just another project that has a definite goal and begins at one point, and ends, shortly after, at another. In a strong democracy, engagement—citizen-to-citizen and citizen-to-school—is the norm, not a one-time venture.[14]

Public Building in Suggsville

What would engagement look like if it were citizen-initiated and community-based? Where is that happening? The foundation doesn't have a list of model communities where everything that citizens should do is being done. Democracy is not perfection; it is too much a human enterprise. Examples of citizens engaging one another crop up in different locations. Some communities provide clear illustrations of citizens naming problems in their own terms. Others offer powerful examples of collective decision making, and so on. Even if there were a list of models, copying them would not be consistent with the way a democratic citizenry goes about its business. Imitation doesn't generate political energy.

---

[14] Benjamin Barber introduced me to the term "strong democracy." All of his books have been helpful, particularly those on civil society, citizenship, and the politics of education. In the context of this book, I would recommend reading *A Place for Us: How to Make Society Civil and Democracy Strong* (New York: Hill and Wang, 1998) and *An Aristocracy of Everyone: The Politics of Education and the Future of America* (New York:Ballantine Books, 1992).

In order to paint a picture of what public-building engagement looks like, I've created a composite community based on cases the foundation has studied. And I have intentionally drawn from places where conditions were less than ideal to reflect the difficulties in public engagement. This composite town is Suggsville.[15]

Suggsville is rural and poor. Once a prosperous farming community, the town began to decline during the 1970s, as the agricultural economy floundered. By the 1990s, the unemployment rate had soared above 40 percent. With little else to replace the income from idle farms, a drug trade now flourishes. A majority of Suggsville's children are born to single teenagers. The schools are plagued with low test scores and high dropout rates. Everyone who could leave the town has, especially the young adults who are college educated. Making matters worse, the community is sharply divided: rich and poor, black and white.

As in other communities facing similar problems, the citizens of Suggsville are worried because *their* property values are dropping, *their* careers are affected, and *their* children are going to schools with fewer and fewer resources. After church and in the one grocery store that has survived, Suggsvillians discuss what is happening with friends and neighbors. People make small talk and mull over what others say.

Then, outside agencies, including several universities, set up programs offering social services, job training, and other assistance. Little changes, however; consultants complain that when they leave, Suggsville goes back to business as usual.

One university group, however, realizes that the problem isn't having the right program; it is having the right strategy. They decide that the best thing to do is to back off and try to put worried, frustrated citizens in touch with one another. No one uses the term *public building,* but that is what is about to take place. Some people are ready to talk to more than family and friends. They want to make sense of their problems, decide what to do about them, and join forces to act.

---

[15] The communities used to form the "Suggsville" composite are described in Vaughn L. Grisham Jr., *Tupelo: The Evolution of a Community* (Dayton, OH: Kettering Foundation Press, 1999) and Joe A. Sumners, with Christa Slaton and Jeremy Arthur, *Building Community: The Uniontown Story* (Dayton, OH: Report to the Kettering Foundation, 2005). Also see the Kettering publications *What Citizens Can Do: A Public Way to Act* (Dayton, OH: Kettering Foundation, 1999) and *Making Choices Together: The Power of Public Deliberation* (Dayton, OH: Kettering Foundation, 2003).

Even though outside agencies are available to call on, Suggsvillians eventually decide that no one can solve the town's problems unless its citizens take matters into their own hands.

Though determined to remain in the background, the group from the university helps organize a series of meetings so people can assess the town's situation and figure out what can be done about their problems. (Scholars would say that convening the meetings is providing a "public space" in which people can do the work of citizens.)

The university's invitation for the residents of Suggsville to meet and talk about the community draws the predictable handful. People sit in racially homogeneous clusters—until the chairs are rearranged in a circle and they begin to mingle. After participants get off their favorite soapboxes, tell their own stories, and look for others to blame, they settle down to identifying the problems that concern almost everyone. Economic security is at the top of the list. Rather than spending their time wishing for some industry to relocate in Suggsville, the group picks up on a suggestion that they start locally. They turn their attention to a restaurant that has opened recently; it seems to have the potential to stimulate a modest revival downtown. Unfortunately, that potential isn't being realized because unemployed men (and youngsters who like to hang out with them) are congregating on the street in front of the restaurant and drinking. Customers shy away.

At the next town meeting, the attendance is larger, and people begin to talk about what can be done to save the restaurant. The police chief argues that the problem is obviously loitering and proposes stricter enforcement of the relevant ordinances. Others hesitate, not because they think the police chief is wrong, but because they have different concerns. A woman suggests that the loitering is symptomatic of a more fundamental problem—widespread alcoholism. A man proposes that a chapter of Alcoholics Anonymous be established. Where will it meet? Someone offers a vacant building free of charge.

As these conversations go on over time (one meeting never accomplishes much of anything), the definition of the problem continues to change as people dig deeper into what is happening in front of the restaurant. Some think there are too many youngsters with too little adult supervision and nowhere to go after school. Community members respond with offers of things they are willing to do if others will join them: organize a sports program, provide after-school classes, expand youth services in the churches, form a band. Suggsville is beginning to invent its future by drawing on local resources and the public work that citizens are willing to do with other citizens. The revival started with a small project, but the work soon draws in more people and new organizations.

As the meetings continue, several people argue that encouraging local businesses is fine, but it will never provide enough jobs to revive the economy. Suggsville has to attract outside investment, they insist. Others quickly point out that the center of town, especially the park, has become so unsightly that no one would put a business there. The town needs a facelift. Suggsville's three-member sanitation crew, however, has all it can do just to keep up with the garbage collection. Do people feel strongly enough about the cleanup to accept the consequences? They do. After one of the forums, a group meets and people commit themselves to gathering at the park the following Saturday with rakes, mowers, and trash bags. The work of cleaning up the park begins to accomplish more than removing trash. It creates a stronger sense of community.

During most of the meetings, the recently elected mayor sits quietly, keeping an eye on what is happening. The forums began during the administration of his predecessor, and the town's new leader has no obligations to the participants. In fact, he is a bit suspicious of what they are doing. But no one makes any demands on the town's government, although some citizens probably think it strange that the mayor hasn't offered to help with the cleanup. Before Saturday arrives, however, he sends the town's garbage crew to the park with trucks and other heavy equipment to do what the tools brought from homes can't.

Over the next two years, the ad hoc forum group organizes into a more formal Suggsville Civic Association. New industry doesn't come to town, but the restaurant holds its own. Drug traffic continues to be a problem; still, people's vigilance, together with more surveillance by the police department, reduces the trade. The crowd loitering on the streets melts away. The public school isn't directly involved in any of the economic development projects, but it benefits from the changes in the civic environment. A new summer recreation program becomes popular with young people, and teenage pregnancies decrease a bit, as do dropouts.

Once the association became an official body, some of the time that had been spent on the project is drained away by unproductive organizational disputes. And, as might be expected, some of the association's projects don't work as planned. Nonetheless, citizens adjust their strategies and launch more initiatives. Perhaps this momentum has something to do with the way the civic association involves the community in evaluating projects—and the community itself. The association convenes meetings in which citizens can reflect on what they have learned, regardless of whether the projects have succeeded or not. Success isn't as important as the lessons that can be used in future projects.

Although Suggsville wouldn't make anyone's list of model communities, the town has increased the capacity of its citizens to influence their future. Asked what the two years of public work had produced, one Suggsvillian said, "When people banded together to make this a better place to live, it became a better place to live."[16]

The Language of Public Building

Before going directly to the next section, which analyzes the nature of the public work that citizens do in communities like Suggsville, I want to define the terms Kettering uses to describe the various tasks that make up public work. The names the foundation has given these tasks can give the impression that we are talking about special skills or techniques when, in fact, we aren't.

Take the task of describing a problem that needs attention. People do that in conversations while waiting for a bus or sitting in local restaurants. These conversations revolve around ordinary questions: What's bothering you? Why do you care? How are you going to be affected? Kettering wanted to find a term that would describe what was going on politically when people were trying to identify a problem. As you saw in the Introduction, we have called it "naming."

Recall how the citizens of Suggsville found several ways of describing the problems affecting the restaurant; the names or descriptions ranged from loitering to alcoholism to children without

---

[16] A similar comment was actually made by a citizen from the Naugatuck Valley community in Connecticut. Jeremy Brecher, "'If All the People Are Banded Together': The Naugatuck Valley Project," in *Building Bridges: The Emerging Grassroots Coalition of Labor and Community*, ed. Jeremy Brecher and Tim Costello (New York: Monthly Review Press, 1990), p. 93.

supervision. Those names captured people's experiences and the concerns that grew out of those experiences. Naming the problems was the first step toward becoming engaged.

As people become comfortable with the description or name of a problem, they raise more questions: What do you think we should do about the problem? What did the folks in our neighboring community do? Citizens try to get all their options on the table so they can consider the advantages and disadvantages. Kettering would say that these conversations create a framework for considering the problem. A "framing" collects and presents options for acting on a problem.

Once the options for acting are on the table, a decision has to be made. And that can be done in any number of ways—by voting, by negotiating a consensus, or by deliberating. If decision making is done by citizens weighing the possible consequences of a decision against what is deeply important to people, Kettering would call that "public deliberation." The term may sound a bit strange, even though it is used to describe what juries are supposed to do. Outside juries, you can hear deliberation taking place as people ask one another: If we did what you suggest, what do you think would happen? Would it be fair? Would we be better off? Is there a downside? If there is, should we change our minds about what should be done?

To make deliberation less abstract, consider this story. Before there was e-mail and places for people to talk in coffee shops, the discussions often went on in the lobby of the local post office. (They still do in my hometown.) Glenn Frank, a journalist, recalled the "original and independent . . . thinking" that went on in these "free-for-all discussions." Although people might wear ready-made clothes, their views, Frank said, were "personally tailored." And as they laid "their minds alongside the minds of their neighbors," they "made up the public opinion of the village."[17] That was public deliberation.

Decisions have to be implemented. In Suggsville, people pledged their support and promised to show up for projects. That is "making commitments" in the Kettering lexicon. Implementation results in "public acting," a term Kettering has used to describe a particular type of collective effort that continues over a long period of time and employs the varied resources that citizens have at their command.

[17] Glenn Frank, "The Parliament of the People," *Century Magazine* 98 (1919): 402.

Acting is typically followed by some type of assessment or evaluation. Some communities are intent on measuring their impact in hopes of convincing skeptics that their efforts have had a demonstrable effect. Others are also interested in what they can learn from the totality of their efforts. In addition to measuring immediate effects, they want to evaluate their performance as a community. When what the community learns about itself is part of the assessment, and the citizenry itself is doing the evaluation, Kettering would say that collective or "civic learning" is going on.

———— ❖ ————

The next chapter will describe how the ordinary ways that communities go about naming problems, framing issues, making decisions, and so on can be turned into practices that engage citizens and allow them to do public work.[18] Routines carried on in ways that facilitate public building are called democratic or public-friendly practices. Let me emphasize again that these practices don't require special skills or techniques. They are variations of everyday community routines.

---

[18] Earlier, I cited two Kettering reports on some of the communities the foundation has heard from: *What Citizens Can Do* and *Making Choices Together.* More accounts of public work are available in the foundation archives of the community politics and leadership workshops.

CHAPTER SIX
PRACTICES THAT EMPOWER

Since democratic practices can be grafted onto existing routines, *communities don't have to do anything outside the ordinary—they just have to do the ordinary in different ways.*[1] In this chapter, I'll discuss six democratic practices, the first three being fundamental because they open the political process to citizens. When people work as a public, they name problems, frame issues, and make decisions in ways that empower them to act collectively.

The Fundamentals

1. Naming Problems in Terms of What Is Most Valuable to Citizens

One of the first tasks in public work is to name the problem that needs attention; that is, to describe it in a way that is meaningful to the people who need to respond. As people give names to problems that reflect their experiences and deepest concerns, a routine activity is transformed into a democratic practice. Everyone becomes a stakeholder. Public terms are distinctive in that they capture invaluable intangibles. Crime can be described in statistical terms, but people value safety or being secure from danger. And there is no number for safety. Recall what happened in Suggsville. The police chief wasn't wrong when he described the restaurant's problem as loitering. But loitering wasn't all that was involved. Because of the forums, citizens added names that were meaningful to them. Suggsville eventually named the problem in ways that captured a number of concerns and experiences. So the naming became a democratic practice.

---

[1] In reporting on democratic practices, Kettering found that practices were being confused with various process techniques. Better group techniques can be useful, but the foundation isn't studying them. Kettering is looking into the basic functions of all bodies politic. Naming problems, for example, is not a special technique; it is a primary function of a body politic. All societies name problems, just as all human bodies feel pain. We don't get to pick and choose among the primary functions that keep us alive personally or politically.

The names that people give problems reflect concerns that are deeply important to most everyone. We all want to be free from danger, secure from economic privation, free to pursue our own interests, and treated fairly by others—to mention a few of these primal motives. Our collective or broadly political needs are similar to the individual needs that Abraham Maslow found common to all human beings.[2] They are more basic than the interests that grow out of our particular circumstances (which may change). And they are different from "values," which also vary.

Some individual needs are quite tangible (food for instance); others (being loved) are intangible. The same is true of the collective needs that motivate us. A few years ago, I was in a community that was facing corruption in high places and egregious crimes on the streets. When citizens asked themselves what they valued most, virtually all said that, more than anything else, they wanted to live in a place that made them proud. Pride is an intangible aspiration rarely mentioned in planning documents or lists of goals. Yet the need to be proud of this city was a powerful political imperative.

I need to make two crucial distinctions here: First, naming a problem in public terms isn't the same as describing it in everyday language. Public terms identify what I just called primal motives or imperatives. These are the things people consider essential to their shared future, the ends or purposes of life, and the means necessary for achieving those ends. Because we all have the same basic political needs, naming problems in terms that reflect them enables people to see their community's difficulties in ways that capture the concerns of most all citizens. That happened in Suggsville when people enlarged the conversation about protecting the restaurant.

Second, naming problems in public terms doesn't result in a one-dimensional description. Many names are used because there is always more than one concern at stake. That was evident in Suggsville when the names for the problem multiplied. "Economic security" was the first name of the town's problem, but then people added others like promoting family and community stability. Although people use different names for different concerns, all of the names come back to things that are essential to their collective well-being.

---

[2] Milton Rokeach and Sandra J. Ball-Rokeach, "Stability and Change in American Value Priorities, 1968-1981," *American Psychologist* 44 (May 1989): 775-784.

Public names facilitate public work because the names encourage people to own their problems, and owning problems is a potent source of political energy. Notice that when citizens in Suggsville added their names for the problem of protecting the restaurant, they tended to implicate themselves in solving their problems. People could do something about the alcoholism that was threatening both the social order and families. And they could do something about the children who suffered when adults took little responsibility for their well-being.

Professionals, on the other hand, name problems in ways that mirror their expertise and the solutions their professions provide. For the police chief in Suggsville, "loitering" was exactly the right name for the problem that threatened to put the restaurant out of business. But it wasn't the only name. I recall Wendell Berry's story of an economist explaining that it was cheaper to rent land than buy it, only to be challenged by a farmer who pointed out that his ancestors didn't come to America to be renters.[3] The economist was technically correct, but the name of the problem wasn't just profitability. The farmer had additional concerns about maintaining a way of life he valued and the independence that owning land provided. Such concerns may not be readily apparent, however; they can't be determined simply by interviewing individuals. People have to talk to one another to sort out what is most valuable to them collectively.

Even though nothing is wrong with professional names, they don't normally take into account what citizens experience. For example, when people look at drug abuse, they tend to think of it in terms of what they see happening to families and the cultural norms that influence young people, not in terms of police interdiction of the drug trade. Even though professional names are accurate, they can be so expert that they create the impression that no other names are possible. When that happens, people don't see their worries reflected in the way problems are presented, so they back off. Furthermore, professional descriptions may give the impression that there is little that citizens can do. The names political partisans use to describe problems aren't professional, yet they can have the same effect. Battles over the right name threaten to ignite conflicts that many people believe are counterproductive.

Public naming helps people recognize what is really at stake in an issue. And when that happens, citizens are more likely to join forces.

[3] Wendell Berry, *The Unsettling of America: Culture and Agriculture* (San Francisco: Sierra Club Books, 1986), p. viii.

Naming problems in public terms can set off a chain reaction leading to collective decision making and action.

As the Kettering Foundation shared its findings on the pivotal role of public naming, we discovered that we were unintentionally contributing to a misunderstanding. Naming isn't a technique that has to be mastered as a special skill would. For problems to be named in public terms, it's enough for people to tell one another how they are personally affected by a problem and what they consider important. As reported in Chapter 5, asking, what bothers you? or some variation of that question often prompts people to begin identifying names. Admittedly, when a tough problem hits a community, discussing what is truly important or at stake before taking sides or debating solutions takes some patience, but it doesn't require adhering to a formula.

Perhaps the most valuable insight that comes from people naming problems in their own terms isn't in the name itself, but in the realization that people already know something about the problems. They can see how the problems affect what they consider valuable. The insight (or "aha") that we can draw valid knowledge from our collective experience is self-empowering. As the saying goes, we may not know how to make shoes, but we know if the ones we have on pinch.

When Americans name problems in terms of their own experiences, they also begin to realize that they are already participating in politics —the politics of solving problems. They don't have to be roused or enlisted, and the political world is less like a far-off planet inhabited exclusively by officeholders and policy experts.

2. Framing Issues to Identify All the Options

After a problem has been named, various options for dealing with it are put forward. When all of these options or approaches to a problem are laid out, they create a framework for decision making. That framework may or may not help citizens make sound judgments. Sometimes an issue is framed around a single plan of action to the exclusion of all others. That kind of framework tells citizens to take it or leave it. Another common framework pits two possible solutions against each other and encourages a debate between advocates. Neither of these frameworks promotes the kind of collective decision making that leads to public work. Public decision making is better served by a framework that includes all the major options (usually three or four). These options grow out of various concerns, which are reflected in the names people use. When the framing reflects the full range of experiences citizens have with an issue and is based on the names citizens have selected, it becomes a democratic practice.[4]

The everyday question, "If you are that concerned, what do you think should be done?" starts the process of creating a public-friendly framework. People usually respond by talking about both their concerns and the actions they favor. Typically, the concerns are implicit in the suggestions for action.

Each concern usually generates a variety of proposals for action. For instance, in a poor neighborhood hit hard by a rash of burglaries, most people would probably be concerned about their physical safety, which is surely a basic political motive. Some might want more police officers on the streets. Others might favor a neighborhood watch. Even though each of these actions is different, they all center around one basic concern—safety. In that sense, they are all part of one option, which might be characterized as protection through greater surveillance. An option is made up of actions that have the same purpose or that take a community in a particular direction.

In the kind of neighborhood I've just described, there are likely to be worries other than physical safety. These might include concerns about economic deprivation and declining norms of social responsibility. Each would generate its own proposals for action. As in the matter of safety, reviving the economy would stimulate a variety of proposals. So would restoring a sense of social responsibility. And each cluster of actions, centered on its own underlying concern, would make up an option for dealing with the overarching issue, which might be something like "neighborhood revitalization." The sum of the options is the framework.

When people are explaining their concerns and describing what should be done about each of them, it is sometimes difficult to realize that different actions actually belong in the same option because the motivations behind the actions are more implied than explicit. During the Cold War, the United States was presented with what appeared to

---

[4] Kettering has seen numerous instances where citizens have framed issues in order to increase their chances of making sound decisions. Cases of other deliberations that have led to civic action are reported in such Kettering publications as *What Citizens Can Do: A Public Way to Act* (Dayton, OH: Kettering Foundation, 1999) and *Making Choices Together: The Power of Public Deliberation* (Dayton, OH: Kettering Foundation, 2003).

be different options for defense: use satellites to detect incoming missiles, protect U.S. missiles in underground silos, or place mobile missiles on naval vessels and airplanes. Although different technically, all of these courses of action were based on one underlying imperative: maintain our superior military strength. So the different actions that would give us military superiority were all actually part of the same option. Of course, this wasn't the only option to consider. People valued strength, but they also valued being on good terms with potential adversaries. So another option included actions that furthered peaceful relationships, such as cultural exchanges and trade. Still another option reflected the conviction that if any one party feels threatened, it is a danger to all other parties. This option, called "mutual security," promoted equality or parity of force and included actions such as arms reduction.[5]

I am trying to illustrate how the things people hold dear lead to different options for dealing with a problem. When all the options, including their downsides, are included in a framework, it creates a basis for the kind of fair trial that engages citizens. For the trial to be fair, each option also has to be put with its best foot forward, with equal attention given to its drawbacks.

Take the issue of protecting the American family. When people consider all of the pressures on today's families, many focus on the importance of the institution of marriage and lament the high divorce rate. These same people may also feel strongly about parental responsibility. And most of them probably worry about what is happening to children when they hear stories of abuse or lack of medical care; they believe in protecting the young. So on just this one issue, people value several things: marriage, parental responsibility, and the well-being of children. Each of these concerns suggests a different option for acting on the problem.[6]

Playing out the example, imagine a community that wants to strengthen its families in the face of increasing juvenile violence,

---

[5] Public Agenda Foundation with the Center for Foreign Policy Development at Brown University, *The Superpowers: Nuclear Weapons and National Security*, National Issues Forums (Domestic Policy Association, 1987).

[6] This account of what happens during deliberations on how to save American families was based on the outcomes of NIF forums on that issue. See Doble Research Associates, *The Troubled American Family: Which Way Out of the Storm?* NIF Report on the Issues (National Issues Forums Institute, 1996).

child neglect, teenage pregnancies, and divorce. Lacking the money to respond to all of these problems, the town council needs to identify the interventions most likely to be effective. The council calls for town meetings to weigh the tradeoffs that will have to be made.

As citizens frame the issue to identify options, one option they might see immediately (because of strong feelings about marriage) would be to try to reduce the high divorce rate. An action consistent with this option would be to use the town's budget to set up a marriage-counseling center. The downside, however, might reflect another widely held conviction about the importance of privacy. Some people would probably say that marriage is a private relationship; governments should not intrude.

A second option that citizens might put on the table could grow out of concerns about parental responsibility. Actions consistent with this option could range from using council funds for courses on parent-ing skills to instituting mandatory jail sentences for parents who fail to supervise their youngsters. Once again, though, a parent-centered policy might trigger the same objections as a marriage-centered policy —government intrusion into private life.

A third option could follow from the conviction that children have to come first; they must be protected from the things that put them at risk, such as violence and drugs. This option might be implemented by offering anger-management courses in the schools or assigning more undercover policemen to arrest drug dealers. Or the council could focus on street gangs and get tougher on youth offenders. The downside? All of these measures are controversial for a variety of reasons. For instance, some people would object to using schools for purposes other than teaching the basic academic subjects. And there would surely be differences of opinion over putting young people in jail.

This is not to suggest that town meetings will be free of disagree-ments if issues like this one are presented fairly by showing the pros and cons of each option. Everyone may share many of the same concerns yet weigh them differently. For instance, on the issue of strengthening families, those who are concerned about privacy and wary of government intervention may also have strong feelings about the need to hold parents responsible. When citizens face issues squarely, they can't escape the pull and tug of the things they value most. Framings have to capture these tensions.

Making choices inevitably requires people to sort out what is most valuable to them—not valuable in the abstract, but valuable in specific situations. The real world context is critical and has to be considered in the framing. Is it more important for the town to care for children than to go after irresponsible parents? What is actually happening in the community? Knowing that there are already a number of agencies with effective programs for young people but that cases of parental neglect are increasing would certainly influence people's decisions.

3. Deliberating Publicly to Make Sound Decisions

In the community concerned about family stability, the town council could have decided which policy to adopt on its own. Or it could have negotiated a settlement with stakeholders like the local social service agencies. Decision making is a routine political activity, and on some questions, elected representatives should decide. On other matters, the decision making needs to include the citizenry, particularly when problems require civic as well as government action.

Keep in mind that citizens make different kinds of decisions than the solution-specific conclusions that officeholders have to reach. Citizens decide on ways to approach a problem; they aren't usually in a position to decide technical matters. The options in a public framing are more than solutions.

It is no secret that public matters are often decided without citizens having to make any difficult choices. People may present their needs or describe the future as they hope it will be but not participate in deciding how their needs are going to be met or how their wishes are going to be realized. And the question of what they can do, themselves, never comes up. Yet if decision making is to become a public practice, something has to happen in communities—more than letting people describe what they want or negotiating with stakeholders. Collective decision making has to be open to the public, and deliberation can open it.

Recall that deliberation is weighing the likely consequences of various approaches to a problem against all that we consider truly valuable. It increases the probability that a decision will be sound by helping a community determine whether the actions being considered are consistent with what people consider most important for their collective well-being. Although we can't be certain we have made the right decision until after we have acted, deliberation forces us to anticipate costs and benefits, to ask how high a price we would be willing to pay in order to get what we want. In the community that wanted to strengthen families, citizens had to weigh protecting children against their reservations about government interference in private life. They had to decide which was more important.

Public deliberation doesn't require any special skill; it is a natural act. Citizens deliberate on personal matters all the time with family and friends. And people are attracted to public deliberative decision making because their experiences and concerns count as much as professional expertise and data.

Sound decisions certainly require sound knowledge, but there is more than one kind of knowledge, particularly for the questions citizens face, which can be answered in more than one way. Knowing which answer is best for a community requires a knowledge that can't be found in books because the questions aren't just about facts. The questions are ultimately about what *should* be. People have to determine what the facts *mean* to them as a community. And people have to create the knowledge needed to respond. This means that public knowledge has to be socially constructed. A more accurate term for this sort of knowledge would be "practical wisdom," or sound judgment. When citizens deliberate with one another, they develop this kind of wisdom or judgment. Deliberation, the ancient Greeks explained, is "the talk we use to teach ourselves before we act."[7]

Campaigns to educate citizens should take note. What the public needs to know—and the way a citizenry goes about knowing—are different from what professionals know and the way they go about knowing.[8] Factual information is no substitute for the talking that peo-

---

[7] Isocrates described practical wisdom in his "Antidosis." Isocrates, "Antidosis," in *Isocrates*, trans. George Norlin, vol. 2 (1929; reprint, New York: G. P. Putnam's Sons, 2000), pp. 179-365.

[8] For more on the relationship between expert and public knowledge, see Robert A. Beauregard, "The Public Negotiation of Knowledge," *Higher Education Exchange* (1998): 16-20 and William B. Lacy, "Democratizing Science in an Era of Expert and Private Knowledge," *Higher Education Exchange* (2001): 52-60. Also see a chapter I wrote for the Kellogg Forum on Higher Education for the Public Good, "Listening to the Public: A New Agenda for Higher Education?" in *Higher Education for the Public Good: Emerging Voices from a National Movement*, ed. Adrianna J. Kezar, Tony C. Chambers, and John C. Burkhardt (San Francisco: Jossey-Bass, 2005). Donald A. Schön distinguished expert thinking from other ways of knowing in *The Reflective Practitioner: How Professionals Think in Action* (New York: Basic Books, 1983) and in *Educating the Reflective Practitioner: Toward a New Design for Teaching and Learning in the Professions* (San Francisco: Jossey-Bass, 1987).

ple must do to teach themselves. Making sound decisions requires the exercise of human judgment to determine the consistency between proposed actions and what is valuable to people.

This isn't to say that expert knowledge is unimportant; it is necessary, though not sufficient. Factual information, along with personal experience, describes the circumstances that require a decision to be made. And the circumstances have a bearing on the soundness of a decision. Driving at the speed limit makes sense if the roadway isn't crowded and the surface isn't slick. But if the surface is covered with freezing rain and the traffic is heavy, driving at the speed limit may not be a sound decision. Citizens pay a great deal of attention to circumstances when they deliberate. For instance, they begin to read and listen to the news more.

Deliberation and Democracy

Public deliberation is a different way of doing politics, not just a different way of talking (although talking is a political act: to talk fear is to frighten, to talk reconciliation is to reconcile).[9] And deliberation doesn't necessarily require holding a special meeting called a "forum"; it can occur anywhere collective decisions are made. To deliberate is to work together in a different way. That is why collective decision making has aptly been called "choice work"; it is real work with specific tasks to accomplish. Here are some of them:

To Move beyond First Reactions and Popular Opinion

The warning "act in haste, repent at leisure" applies to communities as well as individuals. The first job of public deliberation is to help communities get beyond first impressions to more shared and reflective opinions, or what some call "public judgment." Public judgment is not the same as popular opinion, which is often contradictory and short-sighted.[10] Deliberation combats polarization, knee-jerk reactions, emotional meltdowns, misperceptions of the problems at hand, and a failure to understand other people.

[9] Michael and Suzanne Osborn described the politics involved in "participative communications" in *Alliance for a Better Public Voice* (1991). This book was designed for educators in speech communication and published by the Kettering Foundation on behalf of the National Issues Forums Institute.

[10] The term "public judgment" was coined by Daniel Yankelovich in *Coming to Public Judgment: Making Democracy Work in a Complex World* (Syracuse: Syracuse University Press, 1991).

Are Americans willing to accept the consequences of a popular course of action? No one can know until people have faced up to the cost and the long-term effects. Deliberation can help them do that. Suggsville's deliberative forums certainly moved the community beyond the first reaction to the restaurant's difficulties—arrest the people loitering—to a more thoughtful and inclusive analysis.

To Work through Strong Emotions

Another task of deliberation is to deal with the emotions that are always a part of decision making. Public deliberation is more than a purely rational exercise in critical thinking; emotions are involved. When we are confronted with a difficult decision, we usually begin by either denying that there is a real problem or blaming our troubles on somebody else. Emotions inevitably come to the surface; they are generated by the attachment we have to things we consider valuable.

I often use security from physical danger or the need to be treated fairly as examples of things that generate strong feelings. Feelings become intense when what we may need to do to solve a problem threatens the things we hold dear. An action that would make us more secure from terrorism, for instance, might also require limitations on our freedom.

Tensions arise not only among us because we have different priorities but also within us personally because we want to be both free and secure. Deliberation should help us "work through" the anger and frustration that result, not to make the feelings go away but to reach the point at which we are in control of our emotions. "Working through" is the right phrase because that is exactly what happens when we move from denial or blaming others to facing up to the tensions inherent in every public decision. Only then are we in a position to make sound decisions.[11]

Many Americans recognize that sensitive issues spark emotions, and yet they want opportunities to talk about hot topics frankly, provided they can exchange opinions without being attacked personally. People are often curious about what others who aren't like them think, and they look for opportunities to learn from them—even from those with opposing views. Forum participants have given high marks to

---

[11] Daniel Yankelovich discussed his concept of "working through" problems in chapter 17 of his book *New Rules: Searching for Self-Fulfillment in a World Turned Upside Down* (New York: Random House, 1981).

meetings where they could express strong views without others contesting their right to their beliefs.[12]

To Change Perceptions

It would be impossible to estimate the number of bad decisions that have been made as a result of an incomplete understanding of a problem or a misperception of the people affected by it. Part of public deliberation's job is to develop a comprehensive sense of the problems a community faces and the people affected by them.

When forum participants really struggle over difficult choices, they can develop a better understanding of their fellow citizens. That's important because these same people are going to have to work together, and learning about the ways others experience a problem can improve the strategy that a community uses to deal with it. Repeated deliberations may also change people. Participants say they get a better handle on issues; that is, they are able to put particular issues in a larger context and make connections between problems. People then tend to approach policy questions more realistically. Self-interests broaden and connect; shared concerns become easier to see. Citizens may begin to talk more about what we ought to do and see their personal well-being in a larger context.

Those who have been in a number of deliberative forums report becoming more involved in civic activities, perhaps in part because of a better understanding of others. This mutual understanding, I should stress, is a by-product of choice work; deliberation isn't political therapy. People don't deliberate because they want to feel better about themselves or their problems. They deliberate because they want to *solve* problems.[13]

In addition to having a shared sense of a problem and a better understanding of the people who are going to have to solve it, the exchange of perceptions in deliberation is crucial to developing new

---

[12] These are some of the attitudes that the Kettering Foundation has seen reflected in the deliberative NIF forums. Chapter 12 of *Politics for People: Finding a Responsible Public Voice*, 2d ed. (Urbana: University of Illinois Press, 1999) has a more detailed description of this political discourse.

[13] For a more complete account of the public deliberation's effects, see Doble Research Associates, *The Story of NIF: The Effects of Deliberation* (Dayton, OH: Kettering Foundation, 1996); Steve Farkas and Will Friedman, with Ali Bers, *The Public's Capacity for Deliberation* (Dayton, OH: Public Agenda Report to the Kettering Foundation, 1995); and UNM Institute for Public Policy, *A Builder's Guide to Public Deliberation: An Executive Summary of "Understanding Public Deliberation"* (Dayton, OH: Report to the Kettering Foundation, 1995).

insights and reorienting ideas. One of the ways we get outside our own box is to use the perceptions of other people, which come from their experiences. A visiting scholar at the foundation liked to make this point by describing an imaginary bug crawling on a ball. Wherever the bug went, it saw endless space ahead. But if someone lifted the bug above the ball, it would realize that the space wasn't infinite at all; it was really finite. Deliberation's job is to get us off whatever ball we are on.[14]

Getting off the ball or outside the box is the key to the discoveries that characterize what Suzanne Morse called "smart communities."[15] These communities came up with imaginative projects that, although thought improbable, fit a niche that no one else saw. Our favorite example at Kettering is a nearby rural community that revived itself by using an annual sauerkraut festival to attract visitors to its antique shops. Complete with a sauerkraut queen, the celebration draws over 300,000 people from the surrounding counties and states. Who would have believed it!

Imagine a community frustrated by repeated failures to revive its economy. Typically, the same people keep talking to one another— and getting nowhere. They are like the bug. The town's residents keep bringing up the lack of jobs, so they go to the obvious solution— recruit industries to increase employment.

Suppose, instead, this town held deliberative forums where the "usual suspects" who attend meetings were joined by others who had different experiences. A newcomer might report that he once lived in a town that attracted a new industry—but it brought in its own work-force. Although employment statistics improved, most of the locals who had been jobless remained jobless. They didn't have the skills the new employer wanted. Someone else in the forum might have seen a new industry that paid wages so low that people could scarcely live off them. Influenced by these experiences, participants in the forum might

---

[14] Merab Mamardashvili sometimes told this story with a squirrel rather than a bug. That story is in Bernard Murchland, *The Mind of Mamardashvili* (Dayton, OH: An Occasional Paper of the Kettering Foundation, 1991).

[15] Suzanne W. Morse, *Smart Communities: How Citizens and Local Leaders Can Use Strategic Thinking to Build a Brighter Future* (San Francisco: Jossey-Bass, 2004). See the discussions of innovation on pages 62-66 and 207-212.

decide that the lack of jobs, per se, wasn't the problem, the lack of prosperity was.[16]

When people come to see their problems in a different light, they are usually able to identify new actors who can help solve the problems. And as an understanding of the scope of a problem grows, so does the recognition that other resources are needed to respond to it. Take the last example: If the problem were seen as attracting new industries, a recruiter armed with tax concessions might be all that would be required. However, if the problem were redefined more broadly as prosperity, a recruiter alone couldn't handle the job.

To Make Progress When Consensus Is Impossible

Even though people deliberating may change their perceptions of one another or gain a greater appreciation of others' potential as political actors, it won't necessarily eliminate differences of opinion. People have remained at odds even after gaining a better understanding of why others held contrary views. But this is no small gain. Altering people's perceptions of their fellow citizens and of the nature of the problems they face together can unlock a sense of possibility, which is a driving force behind progress.[17]

In a study of public deliberation, Public Agenda found that about half the participants (53 percent) changed their minds as a result of forums. A much larger percentage (71 percent) had second thoughts about their opinions, even though they did not change their minds. More than three-fourths (78 percent) said they encountered viewpoints different from their own and thought those views were valid.[18]

Deliberation isn't a form of conflict resolution per se, but it is depolarizing. Naming problems to recognize the many concerns that people bring to an issue keeps the focus of deliberation from narrowing to one concern that trumps all others. A narrow focus invites

---

[16] Communities have, in fact, redefined their problems in much the way it was done in this hypothetical case. J. Mac Holladay, *Economic and Community Development: A Southern Exposure* (Dayton, OH: Kettering Foundation, 1992).

[17] The Harwood Group, *Meaningful Chaos: How People Form Relationships with Public Concerns* (Dayton, OH: Kettering Foundation, 1993), pp. 11-14, 31-34.

[18] Farkas and Friedman, with Bers, *The Public's Capacity for Deliberation*, p. 17.

conflict. Although public deliberation rarely ends in consensus, it can provide a shared sense of direction to steer public work.

To Locate the Boundaries of the Politically Permissible

Public deliberation's primary task is to make decisions about the work that the public should be doing. Deliberative forums help people recognize when they are responsible for significant parts of their problems. Then they may reason that, if they can create problems, they must have the capacity to manage them more effectively.[19]

Deliberation among citizens can also help officials do their jobs. Listening to the citizenry weigh options and struggle with tradeoffs can be insightful, and hearing citizens name issues can reveal the deeper motives and concerns they share. As people work through conflicts, they can discover what is truly valuable. Elected officials and administrators need this information because it allows them to enter into conversations knowing where people stand on the issues. Public deliberation also helps locate the boundaries of the politically permissible—what people will and won't do to solve a problem. Those boundaries are useful to know, especially when officeholders think they have to cross them.[20]

Watching deliberation is like watching wallpaper peel. It is slow and messy. And it doesn't produce the quantifiable conclusions that polls do. Still, it shows how citizens go about thinking when they struggle with difficult decisions. You might call this public thinking to distinguish it from the way professionals reason or political leaders make decisions. Public thinking isn't a superior form of thinking; it is just another of the distinctive things that citizens do in their work. Public thinking produces public knowledge and promotes sound judgment. Even though understanding this way of thinking is not the same as knowing what the public thinks, officeholders can benefit from understanding how people go about sorting through costs and benefits as they weigh different options for acting.

---

[19] Doble Research Associates, *Responding to the Critics of Deliberation* (Dayton, OH: Report to the Kettering Foundation, July 1996), pp. 52-55.

[20] Each year in Washington, DC, the results from a number of NIF forums on one issue are presented at the National Press Club. Officeholders, including members of Congress, watch video clips from public forums and compare what they hear with the media coverage and the debates in the capitol. This exchange is taped for *A Public Voice*, a public affairs program produced by Milton Hoffman that is aired on approximately 200 PBS stations each year.

From Decision Making to Action and Beyond

Now to the remaining democratic practices used in doing public work: Naming, framing, and deliberating are of little consequence unless something comes of the decisions that citizens make. The next three practices are critical to realizing the full benefits of the practices that precede them. In fact, they carry the first three into the other work that citizens must do.

4. Complementing Institutional Planning with Civic Commitment

Even in communities where citizens have deliberated over an issue and made decisions about what they think should be done, business as usual often takes over when it comes to implementing the decision. Citizens are pushed to the sidelines again. Institutions may acknowledge what people have decided in deliberations but then fall back on the familiar routines of institutional planning. They assume that once the people have spoken, it's time for officials to follow-up. Their plans don't usually include provisions for public work.

Planning makes sense for institutions, but it isn't the way citizens mount collective efforts. The reason is that the resources needed to implement institutional plans are different from those needed to launch public work. If municipal agencies like the ones responsible for street repair or the water supply are called on to follow through on a community decision, they normally have the legal authority, equipment, and personnel to direct the task at hand. The democratic public, on the other hand, can't command people or deploy equipment, and it seldom has any legal authority. So what is the democratic equivalent of planning? It is citizens making commitments to act and then reinforcing those commitments with covenants or mutual promises.

Nothing would have happened after the Suggsville forums if citizens had not stepped forward to suggest an Alcoholics Anonymous meeting, establish after-school programs for young people, and show up with their tools at the park. Making these commitments isn't spontaneous or magical, nor is it done by institutional planning. People step forward because something valuable is at stake and because they see the possibility that they can act. Although citizens don't always do what they intend, they are more likely to follow through when they have committed themselves in public.

Why do people organize patrols on crime-ridden streets when there is no financial inducement or legal obligation? After all, battling street crime isn't just time consuming; it is dangerous. Typically, most Americans can't be coerced into cooperating. They do what they have pledged to do because their fellow citizens expect it of them. And the commitments are often reciprocal; one group promises another, we will do thus and so if you will do thus and so. Those are the mutual promises or covenants I referred to.

Reciprocity builds connections between groups, something that has long been recognized as essential to effective political organizing. The more far-reaching the connections, the more diverse the resources they can bring to bear on a problem.

Public covenants may sound idealistic, but they work. They have their own kind of social leverage.[21] One community leader explained the good attendance at his association's meetings this way: "If you don't show up, somebody will say something to you about it." It isn't uncommon for deliberations to be followed by mutual promises, either at forums or at subsequent meetings. In Sumter, South Carolina, for instance, teenagers held forums on what to do about drug abuse. The meetings prompted participants to commit themselves to prevention projects, which eventually helped some youngsters find jobs and make their way out of the drug culture.[22]

5. Adding Public Acting to Institutional Action

Just as the public has its own distinctive way of moving from decision to action, it also has its own distinctive way of acting. Government agencies often act on behalf of the public, and people often act individually by volunteering for all sorts of civic projects. Both are beneficial, but neither is the public acting. Public acting is made up of a variety of actions taken by citizens who are working together over an extended period of time.

---

[21] More information on covenants is in Daniel J. Elazar and John Kincaid, "Covenant and Polity," *New Conversations* 4 (Fall 1979): 4-8.

[22] This report is from Barbara Brown, who introduced the deliberative forums to the community. Barbara Brown, telephone conversation with Anne Thomason, September 13, 2004.

Public acting is multifaceted, and the actions it includes should be mutually reinforcing. This enables public acting to be coherent without being bureaucratically coordinated. Mutual reinforcement occurs when deliberations result in a shared sense of direction. (To repeat: Communities don't have to agree on the perfect solution, but they must be as clear as possible about the direction they want to follow.)

The case for public acting, however, is more than an argument for cooperation among citizens. Public acting has unique qualities, such as lower "transaction costs" (the cost of getting things done). When groups of citizens have identified overlapping objectives, as they did in the Suggsville forums, their efforts tend to mesh and reinforce one another. That increases productivity; the whole becomes greater than the sum of its parts. Even though public acting requires a degree of coordination (everyone should show up at the park to mow grass on the same day), it isn't administratively regulated and, consequently, doesn't have administrative expenses.

Rather than substituting for official action, public acting supplements it. Consider the way the Adopt-a-Mile initiative has helped counties reduce litter on roadways. Or recall how the fishery in Florala, Alabama (discussed in Chapter 4), motivated students to learn chemistry in the schools. The potential of public acting to reinforce institutional action has also been recognized in the urban reform literature. For instance, Clarence Stone found that citizens in poorer neighborhoods formed alliances that accomplished far more than any institutions alone could.[23]

Public acting is needed most when communities face what some scholars have called "wicked" problems. A problem is wicked when the diagnosis or definition is unclear, the location or cause is uncertain, and any effective action to deal with it requires narrowing the gap between what is and what ought to be—in the face of disagreement about the latter.[24]

Wicked problems are more human than technical and are so deeply embedded in the social fabric that they never completely go away. They

---

[23] Clarence N. Stone, "Linking Civic Capacity and Human Capital Formation," in *Strategies for School Equity: Creating Productive Schools in a Just Society*, ed. Marilyn J. Gittell (New Haven: Yale University Press, 1998), pp. 163-176.

[24] The classic reference on "wicked" problems is Horst W. J. Rittel and Melvin M. Webber, "Dilemmas in a General Theory of Planning," *Policy Sciences* 4 (1973): 155-169.

are as tricky as they are aggressive and vicious. Each symptom exposes another problem in a never-ending chain. These problems take advantage of a diminished sense of community and then further loosen the ties that bind people. The problem conventionally known as the achievement gap in education is an example of a truly wicked problem.[25]

Given these characteristics, conventional strategies of goal setting, planning, and evaluation aren't well suited to responding to wicked problems. When problems are wicked, a shared understanding of the approximate nature of what people are confronting is more important than an immediate solution. In fact, dealing effectively with a wicked problem may depend on not reaching a decision about a solution early on. The ability of citizens to exercise sound judgment in the face of uncertainty is more important than the certainty of experts. Civic commitment trumps a professional plan. Coping with these problems requires sustained acting that doesn't begin at one point and end at another, but continues in a series of richly diverse initiatives.

6. Turning Evaluation into Civic Learning

The sixth practice essential in public work was called "civic learning" in the last chapter. Like all of the other practices, it is distinctive. Civic learning isn't the same as organizational evaluations, but it can be integrated into the regular routines of community assessment. In civic learning, the community itself learns, and the learning is reflected in changed behavior. In other words, the unit of learning is the community itself, and the measure of learning is community change.

After a community has acted on a problem, the people involved want to know whether they have succeeded. It is only natural. Others are quick to judge. The press declares the results to be beneficial, harmful, or inconsequential. There are one-on-one conversations at the supermarket. Outside evaluators may come in to make "objective" assessments. The community itself, however, may not learn a great deal from chance conversations, the media's conclusions, or the professional evaluations.

Although helpful in many ways, conventional evaluations can undermine civic learning by failing to capture the essence of the

---

[25] On the subject of the achievement gap, I recommend Deborah Meier's *In Schools We Trust: Creating Communities of Learning in an Era of Testing and Standardization* (Boston: Beacon Press, 2002).

dynamics that form the core of public building. Citizens are interested in knowing how well they worked together in addition to what they achieved. They have to unpack their motives and experiences themselves in order to learn from one another. The most unfortunate and surely unintended consequence of external evaluations can be to block this type of assessment; evaluators take over, and citizens have little opportunity to learn from one another.

Traditional evaluations can be complemented by civic learning, however. The most significant difference between the two is that both the objectives and the results are on the table for reconsideration when communities learn. That's different from measuring outcomes against fixed, predetermined goals. In civic learning, people may realize that what they first thought was most valuable turned out not to be as important as it seemed.

The citizens of Suggsville could have measured their success by counting customers at the restaurant or the number of arrests for alcohol abuse. Some probably did. But the members of the civic association had even larger objectives, which couldn't be measured. They wanted to overcome the fatalism that had grown up as the town went into decline. And they needed to know how well they worked as a group. So they asked themselves simple but profound questions: What are we learning? Are the things we are doing getting us anywhere? Are we creating the kind of community we want?

When communities learn, they rename, reframe, and decide again—after the fact. Then they make new commitments to act again. They learn by doing. Deliberation is especially important in learning; it teaches people once they have acted, just as it does before. The questions afterward are much the same. What should we do? Should we have done what we did? Was it really consistent with what we thought was most important? Were we wrong about what was important? Civic learning is all of the democratic practices rolled into one.

Before leaving this last practice, I should mention a question Kettering often hears from civic practitioners. The question usually comes up after a fledgling community initiative is well underway. People want to know, how do we keep up the momentum? Democracy's answer is through continually learning. Democracy assumes that ultimately people are their own sovereigns. They must figure out what to do because there is no other sovereign who can tell them. And the way citizens figure out what to do is to learn from their experiences.

Communities that approach their work as a series of experiments —and study those experiments to improve their performance—have an edge on communities that are so wedded to early success that they quit as soon as the results aren't what they want. Communities that are in a learning mode have a better chance of staying the course.

For that reason, civic learning can't wait until the end of a project; it has to go on continuously. It sets the essential tone for public work by constantly inviting the public back into public business. By that, I mean that learning encourages people to make incremental improvements and not be dissuaded when first attempts don't turn out as hoped. Even failure has its uses when people are learning. Learning communities are like those ideal students who read everything assigned and then go to the library to find out more. These communities don't copy a model, follow a case study, or use a formula. Certainly they study what others have done, but they adapt what they see to their own circumstances. (The Wright brothers watched birds fly, but they didn't try to fly like birds. They applied what they observed to fixed-winged craft.) Communities where civic learning flourishes think of imitation as limitation.

An aside: Civic learning might be a practice that professional educators can nurture as catalysts. Educators understand the nature of learning and the conditions that promote it. Their professional knowledge could be useful in structuring a public-friendly environment for civic learning in their community.

Not Six, but One

All six of these practices are part of the larger politics of self-rule. As I've said, they empower lone individuals by organizing them for public work. The secret of their power is that they aren't stand-alone practices; they fit inside one another, the way the wooden *matrëshka* dolls from Russia do. When a community lays out its options for acting on a problem, it continues to mull over the name that best captures what is really at issue. When people deliberate, they usually continue to revise both the framework and the name of the problem.

I mention this interrelationship because of another question the foundation gets from people who learn about democratic practices and want to use them in their communities. They want to know where to begin. Some groups start with naming issues; others begin with deliberative forums. Which practice they choose is not as important as recognizing that the practices are just parts of a larger whole, a democratic way of governing ourselves. In their book on deliberative democracy, Amy Gutmann and Dennis Thompson argued that democratic practices like deliberation belong anywhere and everywhere—in civic organizations, in school boards, in tenants' associations.[26] There is no one right place to begin, but beginning in a democratic fashion is essential if the objective is to strengthen democratic self-rule. Jay Rosen, one of the foundation's adjunct scholars, put the matter succinctly: The way communities enter politics has to be consistent with the politics they want to flourish. As a practical matter, it is unrealistic to try to stop a community in the midst of solving a problem and ask people to start over by renaming the issue at hand. It is probably better to look for opportunities in what is already going on to change the regular routines of naming, framing, and so on, into democratic practices.

A colleague at the foundation who lives in a nearby rural community faced with urban sprawl is trying to identify these opportunities. The issue had already become polarized with developers on one side and preservationists on the other. Few would have joined her if she had tried to stop the meetings. Instead, she made comments that invited her neighbors to consider modifications in what they were doing—changes that would open the way to democratic practices. "Does anyone see another side to this problem?" she asked. "Are there other options we should consider?" "Almost everyone thinks we should do this, but are there any negative consequences we ought to consider?"

—————— ❖ ——————

By going into so much detail about the democratic practices that are used in public work, this chapter may have seemed a digression from the subject of this book—public building for public education. Chapter 8 will try to make that connection. First though, in Chapter 7, I want to expand on a point I just made, which is that the practices, taken together, add up to a different way of governing ourselves, a more public way. Public politics (another name for democratic self-government) brings with it distinctive ways of thinking about everything, from political power to leadership.

---

[26] Amy Gutmann and Dennis Thompson, *Democracy and Disagreement* (Cambridge, MA: Belknap Press of Harvard University Press, 1996).

PART THREE:
PUBLIC POLITICS IN PRACTICE

POLITICS BY THE PEOPLE

IDEAS IN PRACTICE: WHAT PROFESSIONALS AND CITIZENS CAN DO TOGETHER

CHAPTER SEVEN
POLITICS BY THE PEOPLE

When taken together, the six democratic practices used in public work tell a story about how a democracy functions or how citizens go about governing themselves.[1] This story isn't like the conventional account of how our political system works, although it isn't incompatible with that account. Admittedly, it is a story about how politics *should* be; yet it is based on what has actually happened. It is important to see the whole story and not just the practices because this allows us to rethink the way we understand the basic elements of politics, like power and leadership. In this story the public is different and it plays a different role. The tone of politics is different, too, because the story is about problem solving rather than winning political contests. People also have different ways of dealing with one another because they are influenced by the necessity of working together in order to solve common problems. I want to be as explicit as possible about this concept of democracy before going on to describe how the practices serve both citizens and professional educators.

Different "Rules"

I'll start with the way people deal with one another when they are working on common problems. For example, take the work involved in making decisions about how to attack problems. Choice work imposes what might be called "rules of the game" on people. "Rules" isn't exactly the right word, but maybe it will do for now if I say more about what I mean. Rules bring to mind standards of etiquette. Good deliberative forums are too zesty to be polite, however; strong emotions are

---

[1] This concept of politics has been called by various names; "citizen politics" and "deliberative democracy" are two of the most common. For more on the subject, read *The Deliberative Democracy Handbook: Strategies for Effective Civic Engagement in the Twenty-first Century*, ed. John Gastil and Peter Levine (San Francisco: Jossey-Bass, 2005).

always part of the mix. Neither do I have in mind formal written rules like those prescribing acceptable behavior, such as the "no shirt, no shoes, no service" edict enforced in some restaurants. I mean the pragmatic, situational, or work-inspired requirements for getting a job done. If these rules are followed consistently over time, they might become norms and be reflected in community attitudes. Initially, they are just the ways people have of interacting when they are doing public work. Anything people do together, whether it's raising a barn in the old-fashioned way, playing a team sport, or operating a business, generates its own rules. The same is true in this case, and these rules give the politics of public work a distinctive tone or feel.

Kettering first became aware of these implicit rules from reports on forums that dealt with highly controversial issues like AIDS and abortion. When forums begin with an agreement among the participants to work toward making decisions and not just talk about the issue on the table, the discussions are more likely to be deliberative. Securing an agreement on the objectives of a forum (collective charging of the jury) is an effective way to set standards of behavior. If someone tries to derail the deliberations, others will step in to bring the conversations back on track. The people who bring their groups back to problem solving won't appeal to official rules but to the pragmatic, informal ones with comments like, are there other ways to see this issue? The intent of this question wasn't to be polite, but rather to get all of the concerns into a framework that would promote deliberation.

Some rules are established early on when people work to find a name for a problem that incorporates their varied experiences and concerns. For instance, citizens have to at least consider experiences that are different from their own because these experiences have to be taken into account if the name is to mean something to most everyone. People won't work together otherwise. Rules also develop around creating a framework of options. Americans are suspicious of framings that are weighted in favor of one particular course of action. So creating an acceptable framework imposes a standard of fair mindedness.

Of course, there have been forums where deliberation never took place because there was too little structure. Forum participants were just encouraged to talk and listen. No one suggested there was work to be done. At the other extreme, some forum organizers have worried that participants might disrupt the deliberations. That has seldom happened. Yet the worries have caused forum leaders to overstructure meetings. Apprehensive moderators have intervened after every comment, which blocks the person-to-person interaction that makes deliberation productive. Or they have imposed written rules of behavior, which can stifle an honest exchange of opinions.

The work of making difficult choices creates incentives to listen, to consider opposing points of view, to try to judge fairly. So does the work of securing commitments, acting publicly, and learning civically. Every task in public work has implications for the way people deal with one another—if the work is going to get done.

Most of the rules of public work are actually just common sense. And they aren't confined to what happens in public forums. Broad rules are implicit in the attitudes, norms, and guiding principles of what are called high-achieving communities. Not perfect by any means, these communities have been able to manage their difficulties exceptionally well despite limited resources. They have had staying power and a broad base of participation in civic initiatives.

Vaughn Grisham's study of Tupelo, Mississippi, one of these high-achieving communities, provides examples of the larger rules that go beyond forums and grow out of the full range of public work. At one time, Tupelo was called the poorest town in the poorest county in the poorest state of the Union. Small (its population is about 34,000) and located in rural Lee County, the town had no special advantages: no large body of water, no nearby metropolitan center, and no government installation with a large federal budget. Until 1980, there wasn't even a 4-lane highway within 75 miles. By 2003, thanks to Tupelo, the per capita income in Lee County was second only to Madison County, where the state government payroll fuels the economy. During one 13-year period, Lee County added more than 1,000 new industrial jobs per year and even more service positions. The public schools have consistently been rated among the best in the region, and the citizenry owns them.[2]

---

[2] See Vaughn L. Grisham Jr., *Tupelo: The Evolution of a Community* (Dayton, OH: Kettering Foundation Press, 1999), pp. 2-3 and *U.S. Department of Commerce, Bureau of Economic Analysis, CA1-3-Per Capita Personal Income Mississippi, 2003*, http://www.bea.gov (accessed June 27, 2005).

One might wonder whether a strong economy has been the reason for the robust public in communities like Tupelo. Grisham's investigation of the town's progress, however, has shown that public building preceded and paved the way for economic growth. Robert Putnam had the same question in mind when he studied cities in north central Italy. He found that the prosperous regions weren't civic minded because they were rich, but rich because they were civic minded.[3] Most people in Tupelo agree; Vaughn Grisham says they believe their prosperity has been the result of the way the community goes about its business.

The first rule of business in Tupelo was that the public had to have a role in order for the community to solve its problems. This became a guiding principle born out of experience. Public work in Tupelo began in small neighborhoods when people started making collective decisions and acting on them—using their own resources. Eventually, these groups joined forces to attack problems that affected more than one neighborhood. (The Tupelo story, by the way, suggests that the public is not a large mass but rather a conglomeration of small groups, each grounded in local problem solving but capable of joining with other groups on larger issues.) As small groups of citizens in Tupelo began to act on local problems, their efforts eventually changed notions about what "the people" could do. The rules for collective problem solving led to other guiding principles: See everybody as a resource; never turn the work over to agencies that don't involve citizens; build teams.[4]

Tupelo's confidence in the public might not come so easily in every community. Americans can be very critical of their fellow citizens. Taking issues to citizens or, worse, relying on their decisions strikes some as either naïve or downright dangerous. In one town, a woman who had initially advocated greater public involvement in education reversed course. Maybe that wasn't a good idea, she said. "You have so many conflicting opinions about education and problems in general, and we're certainly not experts." Others have recoiled at the thought of airing issues in the community and asking people what should be done because they believe it will only give more power to the most vocal. Better to keep controversial matters quiet, a realtor

---

[3] Robert D. Putnam, *Making Democracy Work: Civic Traditions in Modern Italy* (Princeton, NJ: Princeton University Press, 1993).

[4] These rules reflect the attitudes that Vaughn Grisham found characteristic of Tupelo.

advised, lest disputes erupt that would drive property values down. He couldn't imagine the public marshalling resources and taking concerted action.[5] Leaders with his mindset probably can't be convinced that democracy will work in their communities. They don't have confidence in the citizenry (and citizens may not have any confidence in them).

These reservations about Tupelo's guiding principles may be one of the reasons the town's achievements have been studied more than they have been replicated. Perhaps communities attempting to copy Tupelo have paid little attention to the practices of public work and the rules implicit in them. Or they may have concentrated more on what was done rather than how it was done and by whom. Tupelo has an automobile museum that attracts visitors, and it may have inspired local museums in other communities. But replicating Tupelo's museum wouldn't necessarily stimulate public work or import its rules.

The most basic rule of self-rule is that citizens have to choose what they do; they can't be conscripted into public work. As logical as that rule is, it has been ignored even in instituting one of the most democratic of all the practices—deliberative decision making. Having seen and enjoyed a demonstration forum, some people have gone out and immediately convened one in their community, forgetting that the first decision their fellow citizens have to make is whether they want to hold forums. Democratic practices can't be used *on* people; they can only be used *by* them. How public-building work begins is crucial; citizens have to own their work every step of the way.

Other Sources of Political Power

Politics done by the people instead of for them not only suggests different rules of the game but also suggests different ways of thinking about political power. Power is usually associated with legal or positional authority and money, which comes from having control over resources or people. Another way to think of power is the ability to join forces and form working relationships. This is power *with*, not *over*, and it is generated by democratic practices.

Some people have authority over others; some don't. And those who don't are seen—and often see themselves—as powerless. This perception

---

[5] Doble Research Associates, *A Consumer Mentality: The Prevailing Mind-Set in American Public Education* (Dayton, OH: Report to the Kettering Foundation, 1999), pp. 21-22.

leads to the assumption that those without power can be empowered only by the already powerful. But if one person empowers another, who really has the power? The power people truly own is generated when their experiences, insights, and talents are combined with the experiences, insights, and talents of others. This relational power is an innate and renewable resource; citizens regenerate it when they use it to do public work because the work fosters new relationships. This self-reinforcing cycle continues and can expand, picking up energy like a benign hurricane. New relationships make even more public work possible. And as people work together, they begin to see that they are making a difference. That opens the way to taking more ownership and responsibility, which, in turn, motivates people to do more public work. This may be one of the reasons high-achieving communities have considerable staying power.

Conventional notions about power have been revised, as they were in Tupelo, when citizens demonstrate what they can accomplish by combining their resources. No one has done more than John McKnight and John Kretzmann to show that people, even in the most impoverished communities, can generate their own power. They have documented what can happen when communities consider the collective abilities of people and not just their needs. Power becomes the sum of the capacities of citizens.

Anyone who lives in a community impoverished by a weak economy and sees people ill, homeless, or otherwise burdened by problems not of their own making knows that individuals have serious needs. So it isn't surprising that one of the standard tools in conventional politics is needs assessment. But emphasizing needs, McKnight cautions, tends to have unfortunate political side effects. People lose a sense of what they can do. So he and Kretzmann created "capacity inventories" to identify untapped individual skills and underused community resources. McKnight insists that every person can be seen as a glass half empty or half full. Labeling people with the names of their deficiencies (that is, their needs) obscures the power that can be generated when citizens "express and share their gifts, skills, capacities, and abilities."[6]

---

[6] John P. Kretzmann and John L. McKnight, *Building Communities from the Inside Out: A Path toward Finding and Mobilizing a Community's Assets* (Evanston, IL: Center for Urban Affairs and Policy Research, Neighborhood Innovations Network, Northwestern University, 1993) and John L. McKnight, "Do No Harm: Policy Options That Meet Human Needs," *Social Policy* 20 (Summer 1989): 7.

Seeing power as innate and relational reinforced Tupelo's conviction that local people must solve local problems, another attitude characteristic of high-achieving communities. In an area of western Connecticut hard hit by plant closings, one citizen explained the need to claim local responsibility this way: "All workers have to realize that we're responsible for our own condition. If we don't devote some time to our unions, our political party, our church organization, and the laws being enacted, we'll wake up and find ourselves with empty pension funds, bankrupt companies, disproportionate sacrifices, and a run-down community."[7]

Civic organizations that begin by searching for the one correct answer to a problem have sometimes discovered that there isn't any one solution. Then people realize that they themselves, with their commitment and energy, can be a large part of the answer they have been looking for. Two founders of a clean water project along the Tennessee River explained, "People have to provide their own hope. Nobody's going to come along and make everything all better. It's us. We're the problem; we're the solution."[8] These people were echoing a song from the civil rights movement, "We Are the Ones We Have Been Waiting For." This sense of responsibility is implicit in each of the democratic practices and should grow as people move from naming, to framing, to deliberating, and on.

Leadership from Everyone

Democratic practices also have special implications for leadership. Strong leaders are critical even in a democracy based on self-rule. Nothing happens spontaneously in a community; some courageous souls always have to step out first. In communities that are adept at solving or at least managing their problems, however, a great many people step forward. These are "leaderful" communities, meaning that everyone is expected to provide some initiative.[9] The communities have redefined leadership by making it everybody's business, not just

---

[7] Jeremy Brecher, "'If All the People Are Banded Together': The Naugatuck Valley Project, in *Building Bridges: The Engineering Grassroots Coalition of Labor and Community*, ed. Jeremy Brecher and Tim Costello (New York: Monthly Review Press, 1990), p. 93.

[8] Leaf Myczack, "We're the Solution," *In Context* 28 (Spring 1991): 19.

[9] The Harwood Group, *Forming Public Capital: Observations from Two Communities* (Dayton, OH: Report to the Kettering Foundation, August 1995), p. 5.

the business of a few, and by not equating leadership with positions of authority.

High-achieving communities aren't distinguished so much by the qualifications of their leaders as by their number, their presence throughout the community and, most of all, the way they interact with other citizens. Traditional leaders are usually intent on getting support for decisions they have already made. They may take months to study an issue and make decisions among themselves yet allow the citizenry little opportunity to do the same. Having agreed on a plan of action, they try to convince people of its merits with a barrage of supporting facts and attractive arguments. The authors of the plan may have deliberated over the pros and cons of various alternatives, but citizens haven't. Even if these leaders succeed in selling their proposals, their communities will have only a persuaded population, not an engaged public with the political will to act on its own. Leaders in leaderful communities, by comparison, are skilled in fostering public decision making and work.

Traditional leaders in positions of authority are also typically gate-keepers who control access to money and give or withhold permission for community projects. Leaders in high-achieving communities tend to be door openers who connect people and broaden participation. They look to the community for solutions, not just to an elite of other leaders. Vaughn Grisham is fond of citing the owner of the Tupelo newspaper, George McLean, who told citizens that if they wanted a better community, they would have to do the work themselves.[10] McLean isn't the only leader who has had this insight. In Kansas, another journalist, Davis Merritt, when editor of the *Wichita Eagle*, argued, "The only way ... for the community to be a better place to live is for the people of the community to understand and accept their personal responsibility for what happens."[11]

Political Space without a Street Address

The politics that emerges from the six democratic practices taken together has still another distinctive characteristic—its location. Usually, people have to go to specially designated places to practice

---

[10] Grisham, *Tupelo*, pp. 90-91.

[11] Davis Merritt Jr., December 1992. From the unpublished transcript of the Public Journalism Seminar, conducted by the Kettering Foundation and New Directions for News, p. 9.

politics: the voting booth or the jury box. The democratic practices, on the other hand, can take place almost anywhere: a coffee shop, a parking lot at the grocery store, even at someone's kitchen table. Almost any of the places where people regularly gather can provide this public space. The ideal locations are those that are open to more than one congregation, class, constituency, or membership.

Frontier America had a lot of public space in locations that might seem unlikely settings for community politics. Ad hoc groups created opportunities for deliberation when they called a town meeting to decide whether to build a school or library. Women's clubs provided public space in sewing circles. The importance of this space today has been documented in a study by Ray Oldenburg. Festivals, Little League baseball games, soccer matches, neighborhood parties, and potluck dinners now bring people together. They chat before and after church services; they talk at weddings and funerals; they sound off in bars and bingo parlors. Conversations in these social settings can lead to more formal deliberations, which may be why Oldenburg called these the "great good places" of a community.[12]

Not all of these social activities lend themselves to democratic practices, however. Those that do have particular characteristics. They allow people to get to know one another as citizens as opposed to being known only by reputation—that is, by social status, family background, or institutional position. And they encourage conversations about the well-being of the community as a whole.[13]

I have been particularly impressed by the public space created as a result of the efforts of more than 30 institutes or centers around the country that are dedicated to teaching democratic practices. Many of these institutes have put collective decision making at the center of their workshops. Institutes at Penn State, Hofstra, and the University of Pennsylvania, among others, specialize in helping communities that want to deliberate on educational issues. Nearly all of the centers use the guides in the National Issues Forums (NIF) series, and some also frame their own issues to stimulate deliberation.[14]

[12] Ray Oldenburg, *The Great Good Place: Cafés, Coffee Shops, Bookstores, Bars, Hair Salons, and Other Hangouts at the Heart of a Community* (New York: Marlowe, 1999) and The Harwood Group, *Forming Public Capital*, p. 3.

[13] The Harwood Group, *Forming Public Capital*, p. 3.

[14] For more information on public policy institutes, see the National Issues Forums Institute Web site at http://www.nifi.org.

Civic groups attending the institutes go back home and identify the problems in their communities that could benefit from public work. The center at Ohio State, for example, assisted Cincinnati in organizing more than 150 local forums where citizens decided on ways to foster better race relations in the city. One of the outcomes of this project was the formation of a new citywide association, Neighbor to Neighbor, which was responsible for following up on the forums. Similar projects at other institutes have provided building blocks for new civic architecture in several communities. In Grand Rapids, Michigan, for instance, an ad hoc association of more than 40 organizations has been sponsoring forums on NIF issues each year for more than two decades. These forums have given hundreds of citizens a chance to make collective decisions and act as a public.[15]

An institute in Iowa illustrates how these centers form and then create public space throughout a state. Established by a coalition of organizations that included the association representing teachers, the organization of school boards, and the state department of education, the fledgling institute, called Iowa Partners in Learning, began by organizing deliberative forums on issues important to the future of Iowa. A year later, the institute analyzed results from the forums and presented them to state agencies. Then Partners began assisting communities that wanted the public to be more involved in making decisions on local issues. New members joined the institute—the parent-teacher organization, the League of Cities, the university system, and an agency for rural development within the U.S. Department of Agriculture. Why the interest? Participants in Partners said they were looking for an alternative to confrontational politics—an alternative they found in deliberative politics.[16]

The community organizations served by these institutes didn't necessarily have creating public space as a goal, even though many of their projects have increased opportunities for the public to do its work. The motivation of most organizations has grown out of their

---

[15] For a report on actions that have followed deliberations, see *What Citizens Can Do: A Public Way to Act* (Dayton, OH: Kettering Foundation, 1999) and *Making Choices Together: The Power of Public Deliberation* (Dayton, OH: Kettering Foundation, 2003).

[16] Randall Nielsen, "Improving Education through Community-Building," *Connections* 11 (February 2001): 9-10.

own self-interests. Local libraries, for instance, want to encourage people to read about important issues, and deliberative forums help. Literacy programs use the NIF books not only to teach reading but also to draw their participants into conversations with other citizens. (Professionals in these programs believe literacy is not just a matter of reading in private; rather, it is the ability to join in the political discourse of democracy.) Advocacy organizations use deliberative forums for different reasons. They want to attract people who don't like to be lectured to. Whatever the immediate goal, the net result of these organizational ventures has been to make ordinary space public.

÷

In sum, the politics implicit in the six democratic practices is unique in every way, from where it takes place, to the type of power it generates, to the leadership it develops. This highly democratic understanding of democracy lends itself to imagining new forms of collaboration between citizens and professional educators, as well as between regular citizens and school board members. This collaboration could help build a public capable of taking responsible ownership of the schools and, at the same time, help strengthen the capacity for self-rule. In the next chapter, I want to introduce ways of thinking about this collaboration using examples of what the ideas might look like in practice. I emphasize the ideas because I wouldn't want readers to expect case studies with detailed blueprints of projects they might copy.

CHAPTER EIGHT
IDEAS IN PRACTICE: WHAT PROFESSIONALS AND CITIZENS CAN DO TOGETHER

Many of the people who read *Is There?* were either school board members or professionals in education, and you may recall that they all asked us the same question: If there isn't a public for public schools, what can we do to see that there is one? *Is There?* identified a problem—the lack of public ownership of the schools—but didn't attempt to offer specific remedies. While this is not a how-to book either, it does have something to say about how the ideas in this book can be used to advantage by educators, school board members, and citizens— in collaboration with one another. Stimulating new ways of thinking about old problems can bring about lasting change in both communities and schools.

I know that truly joint ventures with citizens and educators as equal partners have been difficult to launch. The legacy of distrust from past reform projects is hard to overcome. A common complaint from teachers, administrators, and school board members is that people don't show up when the school calls a meeting. But educators and boards are learning how to be more effective. Some have formed boundary-spanning coalitions with community organizations so they won't be the only ones convening meetings. Recall the case in the Philadelphia area where a number of organizations other than schools were involved —the Scouts, the public library, and the local newspaper.[1]

On the other side of the divide, community organizations have had their own share of disappointments. When they have reached out, school officials have pulled back. These incidents follow a familiar pattern. Civic groups say, "We were beginning to work with the schools, but then a new superintendent came in who...." The story ends badly.

---

[1] Harris Sokoloff, "A Deliberative Model for Engaging the Community: Use of Community Forums Can Undercut Special-Interest Politics," *School Administrator* 53 (November 1996): 12-18.

Rebuffed people join the choir of those who complain that educators are indifferent if not hostile when they try to help the schools.

Despite these mutual frustrations, I believe a different kind of collaboration is possible. The key is recognizing the dynamic qualities of the public and plugging into the political energy they generate. Here are some efforts that take advantage of this idea.

Drawing on the Concepts of Public Naming and Framing

Charles Irish, a superintendent in Medina, Ohio, has taken advantage of the power of public framing. He was faced with an overcrowded high school and worried that dividing the existing school would polarize the community. So he encouraged citizens to frame the issue and lay out a range of options, with the advantages and disadvantages of each presented fairly. As a result, the community didn't split into opposing camps but came up with a proposal that addressed the major concerns (several high schools were established but in a central area).[2] The Mechanicsburg School District in Pennsylvania also worked with citizens to frame the issue of whether to build new schools after a tell-and-sell strategy backfired. The public meetings weren't to usurp the power of the board, but they did result in a set of principles that the board found useful in making its decision.[3]

Naming and framing are democratic practices particularly well suited for reconnecting schools and communities, because schools benefit when what appear to be classroom issues prove to be as much or more community issues. Unfortunately, school issues are prone to be narrowly focused. When that happens, citizens aren't as likely to get involved. Renaming/reframing school issues to reveal the community side of problems can break down the isolation of schools and combat the tendency to depend on these institutions to remedy social ills they can't possibly combat by themselves.

People have sometimes discovered the power of public naming almost by accident. I recall a school board member who complained

---

[2] Doble Research Associates, *Expectations and Realities: An Analysis of Existing Research* (Dayton, OH: Report to the Kettering Foundation, January 2004), pp. 29-30.

[3] Harris J. Sokoloff, e-mail message to Connie Crockett, May 9, 2005.

about poor attendance at meetings on school discipline. When he became a district attorney, however, he noticed that town meetings on juvenile crime drew overflow crowds. Despite some differences, school discipline and juvenile crime are related issues. So why were people so much more attentive to one than to the other? Perhaps because of differences in the way the problems were named. The very name "discipline" suggests that the problem is one that the schools should solve. Consequently, only a few citizens feel obligated to do anything beyond finding out what the educators are doing. But, when the antisocial behavior spreads to the streets and into people's homes, it becomes everyone's problem. Naming this problem to reflect that basic concern probably had something to do with the difference in citizens' responses.

Randy Nielsen, at Kettering, has reported on experiments in other communities that have renamed school problems in public terms. He cites a school district in Pueblo, Colorado, that received a large grant to promote health education, which would have added a course on sex education to the curriculum. A controversy over the course soon threatened to polarize the community. Schools were caught in the middle between opposing factions. Because the issue could not be decided, the grant was revoked. Losing the money only intensified the controversy.[4]

With the help of the Colorado Association of School Boards, Pueblo then began a series of community conversations to find out exactly what was troubling people. Surprisingly, given the controversy, the meetings showed that most people weren't as concerned about sex education in the schools as they were about teenage pregnancy in the community. That issue had been masked by the debate over sex education. Pueblo then renamed and reframed the issue. The changes were instrumental in creating an initiative to enlist all the community agencies that could help reduce teenage pregnancies. The experience also illustrates the potential in the idea of naming problems in public terms.

---

[4] Randall Nielsen, "Public Schools and the Practices of Engaged Communities," *Connections* (April 2004): 20. The Pueblo case study is also included in Colorado Association of School Boards, *Public Engagement in Five Colorado School Communities* (Dayton, OH: Report to the Kettering Foundation, 2003), pp. 7-8.

"Auditing" Democratic Practices to Stimulate New Insights

Ideally, all the democratic practices are being used in a community, but what if they aren't? Maybe it would be useful to check up on a community's practices—on how issues are named and framed, on who makes the decisions, on what public acting does or doesn't follow from the decisions, and so on. Schools are audited regularly to be sure they have the financial resources and management systems needed to function effectively. Why not audit a community's capacity to do public work? I don't mean an audit in the sense of a critical review aimed at producing information, but rather a joint citizen/educator examination of the extent to which community routines are open to the public or the extent to which they have become democratic practices. Making the community itself the unit of analysis breaks the habit of concentrating on specific issues isolated from one another. And the audit could open the way to using ideas about public practices.

The National School Public Relations Association (NSPRA) has already begun experimental projects along these lines called "community audits," which are a variation on the association's "communication audits." The new audit asks citizens to consider questions like, what do you value most about your community? What motivates you to get involved in community activities?[5]

As is true of all experiments, the audits have encountered some problems. For instance, some of the participants in the NSPRA project wanted how-to manuals, and these aren't available for experiments. Crises have also interfered, and the audits have tended to stop and start. Nonetheless, these projects have made progress in shifting the focus from the schools alone to the community and have encouraged people to consider other ways of thinking about the public.

One of the NSPRA projects took place in the Cave Creek Unified School District in Arizona. The superintendent, John Gordon, served as a civic leader for an effort that was genuinely based in the community. The school district is in a desert, so land development has to be

---

[5] National School Public Relations Association, *Community Audit* (Dayton, OH: Report to the Kettering Foundation, September 2003).

managed in a way that protects a fragile environment. The school is affected by how issues like water rights and traffic flow are named, framed, and decided. But the superintendent didn't act as a special interest lobbyist for the district. Along with a local foundation and other parties, Gordon used a community dialogue to bring public practices into business as usual. The community had an opportunity to audit these practices as it dealt with the land use issues.[6]

Audits like the one being developed by NSPRA can gauge the use of the practices that result in public work. It shouldn't be difficult to assess a citizenry's capacity for collective decision making and public work. The extent to which the concerns of citizens are reflected in the names given to the major community issues should be easy enough to see. The same is true of how issues are framed and who is involved in making important decisions. And it wouldn't be difficult to check on the degree to which different civic groups come together in complementary public acting. The amount of collective learning that is going on may be trickier to assess, yet not impossible. If a community is using these democratic practices, it is safe to assume that space is being provided for them. The payoff from the audits, however, isn't what they find; it is the ideas they introduce.

Another type of community checkup used to determine whether a community has the sort of problems that can be solved only by public work is called *Hard Talk*. It consists of analytical questions communities can ask themselves.[7] In the tests, people could, indeed, distinguish between those problems that are on the surface, like gum stuck to the bottom of a shoe, and the wicked ones that are embedded in the political, economic, and social fabric of the community. These are the problems that take the proverbial village to solve. Citizens also recognized that these wicked or systemic problems take time to remedy, which requires a public with considerable staying power. This insight might prevent the haste that disrupts the natural process of civic engagement and also demonstrate the need for sustained public acting.

---

[6] National School Public Relations Association, *NSPRA/Kettering Public Engagement Project: Final Report for July 2002-December 2003* (Dayton, OH: Report to the Kettering Foundation, 2003), pp. 5-6.

[7] Bob McKenzie, who studied the effects of *Hard Talk*, reported that people were, indeed, able to distinguish between types of problems. For the questions that were used, see *Hard Talk: Connecting Education with Our Community* (Dayton, OH: Kettering Foundation, 1992).

Hard Talk raised additional questions about the types of actions that are best suited to various problems. For certain difficulties, laws, regulations, and government programs are appropriate. Other problems require citizens to be involved, directly and personally. For instance, local "networks of nurture," or neighbors caring for neighbors, have been found essential in delivering health care.[8] Studies show that these networks have a profound effect on community well-being, even on rates of heart attacks and cancer.[9] In the *Hard Talk* tests, people were able to match problems with appropriate actions. A minister of an inner-city church put it best when he said of wicked problems, "programs don't solve [these] problems, people do."

Checkups like *Hard Talk* and the NSPRA audit encourage democratic practices by identifying conditions where they are essential. That is how they make new ideas about politics available to communities. For instance, the various influences that put young people at risk prove to be beyond the ability of any single agency or group to manage. Like other wicked problems, this one springs from multiple sources and demands attention from multiple actors. Only a combination of forces, both civic and governmental, stands a chance of being effective. To recognize that is to recognize the need for public acting to marshal a variety of resources and use them to complement institutional action.

When communities analyze their problems to identify those that are systemic, that need repeated attention, that require a human touch—problems with multiple causes that must be attacked on several fronts—they should be more likely to see the necessity of a public made up of citizens in motion. These problems move from neighborhood streets into classrooms. They defy our best professionals, confound our most expert experts, and overwhelm our most effective institutions. Despite reservations about involving people, communities have to turn to them when public work is essential.

---

[8] Marc Pilisuk and Susan Hillier Parks, *The Healing Web: Social Networks and Human Survival* (Hanover, NH: University Press of New England, 1986).

[9] The classic study of what citizens can do was done in Roseto, Pennsylvania. There are several sources. I suggest John G. Bruhn and Stewart Wolf, *The Roseto Story: An Anatomy of Health* (Norman: University of Oklahoma Press, 1979).

Tapping into the Appeal of Education as an Idea

One of the characteristics of the public is the way citizens think about education. Earlier in this book, I wrote about the positive attitudes people have about "education" as compared to "schools." This becomes a useful distinction if it can be illustrated in practice. That might happen if communities devised comprehensive strategies for strengthening all of their educating institutions.

Larry Cremin, who is known for his histories of education, once pointed out the anomaly of having boards of *education* that select only superintendents for *schools*. He wasn't suggesting that school boards actually take control of libraries, museums, public television stations, and our other educating institutions. He was simply encouraging people to imagine what might happen if communities broadened their focus from schooling to educating. Conceivably, citizens might form a coalition of all of their educating institutions and call it their "board of education." Such a board might decide on a strategy for educational development, somewhat like those that are routinely devised for economic development. Economic development planning usually involves a number of organizations: Local and state governments are asked to provide a physical infrastructure of roads and utilities; banks and other financial institutions are called on to raise capital; technical schools are assigned the job of training a skilled work force. Why not do something similar to build a comprehensive educational infrastructure including libraries, museums, youth organizations, health centers, and business training programs—along with public schools?

Every strategy is based on a set of objectives, so an educational strategy would have to be grounded in what people decide is best for their communities. And citizens would need to deliberate to determine not only what is best, but also what actions are most consistent with what they hold dear. Then they would have to choose the institutions suited to taking on the various tasks identified in the strategy.

Think of any city where the public schools are losing enrollment as people move to the suburbs. The dropout rate increases—as does joblessness. The existing workforce isn't trained in the skills needed by new industries, which use the latest technologies. No single institution can respond to all of these problems. A comprehensive strategy for this city would have to draw on the resources of all of its educating institutions, formal and informal, much as an economic plan would have to involve all the key economic actors. Instead of acquiring land for an industrial park, an educational strategy might call for the creation of an employment and training center, which would be linked to schools, family services, and employers. Something like this actually happened in Dayton, Ohio. Fred Smith, a local businessman, demonstrated the communitywide impact of workforce development on social service agencies, the police department, businesses, and the schools. Then, he and a group of citizens devised a comprehensive strategy for responding, which involved most of the affected institutions.[10]

Admittedly, a comprehensive strategy for education is more a potential than a reality. In an 11-city survey, Clarence Stone could not find a comprehensive effort that was backed by all segments of a community. On the other hand, he couldn't find a school district without some civic effort and "significant involvement from other sectors of the community."[11]

The insights that education includes but is more than schooling—and that democratic practices can be used to develop a comprehensive educational strategy—have come closest to being implemented by community projects to strengthen what Vaughn Grisham has called their "educational infrastructure." One of these involved Okolona, Mississippi, where, over a period of 15 years, a local citizens' organization, EXCEL Incorporated, opened an after-school program, established summer learning camps, and founded an adult school to teach basic literacy skills. Okolona's educational infrastructure complemented the work of the schools while providing various types of education for a wide range of people in the community.[12]

---

[10] To learn more about the results of this strategy, visit http://www.thejobcenter.org.

[11] Clarence N. Stone, "Linking Civic Capacity and Human Capital Formation," in *Strategies for School Equity: Creating Productive Schools in a Just Society*, ed. Marilyn J. Gittell (New Haven: Yale University Press, 1998), p. 169. John Goodlad has also pointed out the advantages of connecting multiple actors in a systemic strategy. John I. Goodlad, *A Place Called School: Prospects for the Future* (New York: McGraw-Hill, 2004), p. 271.

[12] For more information on Vaughn Grisham's findings, contact the George McLean Institute for Community Development at the University of Mississippi. EXCEL Incorporated (Enrichment in Excellence through Community Education and Leadership) is at 230 W. Main Street, Okolona, Mississippi.

Of course, multifaceted programs like the one in Okolona are not uncommon. What makes them useful in illustrating the concept of public building is when they are the result of public work.

Seeing the Community as an Educator

Okolona appears to be a community that realizes that one of its primary responsibilities, in addition to providing public facilities and a physical infrastructure, is to give its citizens opportunities to grow to their full potential. That recognition can be another foundation for collaboration between educators and citizens.

Unfortunately, not every community recognizes that obligation, even though early on most had a de facto strategy for carrying out this responsibility. Schools and other educational institutions have, at various times, been joined in common causes, which have resonated with the decisions citizens made about the kind of community they wanted. As the years go by, however, and conditions change, schools, libraries, and museums become more independent and their earlier sense of dependence wanes.

In many ways, schools and other institutions of education were created to supplement the education provided by the community, which was the primary educator. That education began in homes (which were the first schools for reading) and radiated through everything from patriotic events to jury service (which instructed people in public virtues and civic responsibility).[13] Edmund Gordon has revived that idea and turned the current assumption that communities should supplement the work of schools on its head.[14] He believes that the schools should supplement the education provided by the community! The notion that the community itself can be a force in education strikes me as useful; it certainly strengthens the case for closer ties between schools and communities.

Sometimes a crisis will remind communities of this interdependence. That happened in the town of Mansfield when the local school was

[13] For an overview of America's early history of education broadly defined, I suggest Lawrence A. Cremin, *Traditions of American Education* (New York: Basic Books, 1977).

[14] See Edmund W. Gordon, Beatrice L. Bridglall, and Audra Saa Meroe, eds., *Supplementary Education: The Hidden Curriculum of High Academic Achievement* (Lanham, MD: Rowman and Littlefield, 2004).

threatened by consolidation. Waiting until there is a crisis, however, is usually waiting too long. Perhaps communities can recall this essential connection by revisiting their history.

Since most educating institutions have their roots in the early histories of their communities, local study groups should be able to find evidence of the school-community connection. Students in a number of towns have already shown the way by doing local history projects with their parents, grandparents, and other community members. Some of these projects have fostered a lasting appreciation for how a community works and the role that the citizenry has played in education.[15]

To test the effects of recalling educational history, two institutes at Auburn University have designed a community project for Alabama.[16] The project has the potential to do more than rescue the history of all the institutions that have educated; it might prompt communities to identify contemporary resources that could be used in education. And it could renew an appreciation for the idea that a community is an educating institution itself.

Using Democratic Practices to Rethink Professional Routines

Throughout this book, I have had a good deal to say about the tension between professionals in education and citizens. Now, I want to recognize their interdependence. That interdependence has already been emphasized by professionals in a number of other fields; they are busy recovering the civic dimensions of their work. These include academics who consider themselves "public scholars" and journalists who

---

[15] Michael L. Umphrey, "Tinkling Cymbals and Sounding Brass: Hearing the Different Drum" (featured author presentation, Montana Education Association/Montana Federation of Teachers Annual Conference, Billings, MT, October 16, 2003).

[16] This project in community educational history is being done through collaboration between the Center for the Arts and Humanities and the Truman Pierce Institute at Auburn University.

created public or civic journalism.[17] Most of these "civic profession-als," as they have been called, respond to a rationale that Dr. Ronald Heifetz, a professor of government at Harvard University, has articulat-ed. Because of his training as a physician, Heifetz knew that medical problems range from the routine, for which a doctor has a ready reme-dy, to the more serious, for which there is no simple diagnosis and no easy technical fix. For instance, there is a technical remedy for a bro-ken arm but not for diabetes. For the most serious problems, patients and physicians have to synchronize their efforts. Other professionals have come to similar conclusions: they need the public in order to do their jobs.[18]

Some professionals in education know they need a responsible public but there isn't one in their community; they are too hard pressed by day-to-day problems to spend time on public building. I can imag-ine at least the broad outline of a type of collaboration that would not take professionals out of their customary routines, yet would increase the capacity of citizens to do public work in education. It involves aligning professional routines with democratic practices.

Admittedly, "aligning routines" sounds vague. It could mean anything from being more communicative to actually bringing citizens into administrative meetings and classrooms. *Aligning could also be a way of thinking about a relationship*, which is a concept, not a regimen of things to do, like dieting. The concept grows out of recognizing that even though professionals are citizens and citizens are often

---

[17] One of Kettering's publications, the *Higher Education Exchange*, has numerous articles on public scholars and other civic professionals. Also see the publications of William Sullivan at the Carnegie Foundation for the Advancement of Teaching, especially *Work and Integrity: The Crisis and Promise of Professionalism in America* (New York: HarperBusiness, 1995). Some professional educators could be included among those who have recognized they can't do their jobs without the public. See Clarence Stone, "Linking Civic Capacity and Human Capital Formation," in *Strategies for School Equity: Creating Productive Schools in a Just Society*, ed. Marilyn J. Gittell (New Haven: Yale University Press, 1998), pp. 163-176. Harry Boytc also reports that "public work has proven a powerful resource for teacher education" in several programs for professional educators being assisted by the Humphrey Institute's Center for Democracy and Citizenship at the University of Minnesota. See "Civic Learning Project: A Project to Strengthen the Civic Dimensions of Teacher Education" (February 2005), p. 4.

[18] Ronald A. Heifetz and Riley M. Sinder, "Political Leadership: Managing the Public's Problem Solving," in *The Power of Public Ideas*, ed. Robert B. Reich (Cambridge, MA: Ballinger Publishing, 1988), pp. 185-191.

professionals, the work of citizens and professionals is both different and similar. Most engagement efforts attempt to do away with those differences by bringing citizens into the world of professionals or by having professionals explain their worlds more clearly to citizens. Aligning professional routines with democratic practices doesn't involve merging these two worlds.

The worlds of professionals and citizens often collide. That is why professionals erect barriers to protect their domains. Aligning suggests keeping the worlds on parallel tracks and maximizing opportunities for mutual assistance. Specifically, the idea of aligning is to carry on professional routines in whatever ways make it easier for citizens to do their work. Then public work can complement the work of professionals.

Earlier in this book, I wrote that citizens name problems, frame issues, decide questions, implement decisions, act, and learn in ways that are different from professionals. Professionals also name, frame, decide, implement, act, and learn. It is almost as if the two lived in the parallel universes found in science fiction movies. In our reality, every democratic practice has its counterpart in a professional routine. Aligning is recognizing this similarity and making use of it in all the varied ways that imagination can suggest.

The chief obstacle to alignment is the perception that what professionals do is purely professional and not political. That is true, in part. Yet it is also true that professional routines have powerful political consequences. For instance, the terms that superintendents use to describe a problem to the community have political consequences. So does the way they frame issues.

The first step in alignment is to be aware that citizens have other ways of naming, framing, and so on. Professionals need to know the names citizens give issues because the names reveal what is truly important to people. That information can improve expert diagnoses. And a professional framing of solutions can be strengthened by knowing what is in a public framing of options. On the other side of the coin, sharing the rationale behind a professional framework with citizens might make people more receptive to the expertise that professionals believe is often discounted. At a minimum, professionals can be sensitive to not using the power of their offices to impede, albeit unintentionally, public work. For instance, professional names of issues can preempt a public framing. And take-it-or-leave-it decisions from on high, even good decisions, discourage citizens, particularly the less-organized ones; they see no way to get involved or make a difference.

I wish Kettering had more research to offer on experiments in alignment. The foundation would like to pursue this matter with those well versed in administrative routines, which Kettering is not. All we can say now, though with conviction, is that better alignment of professional routines and democratic practices should serve both well.

The major difficulty we have seen so far is educators trying to copy rather than to reinforce democratic practices. For instance, aligning professional decision making with public deliberation doesn't mean that citizens should deliberate on matters that are wholly in the province of boards or administrations (budgets, for example). Most people aren't looking to reclaim the work they have delegated to institutions and legislative bodies. But they want to make the kinds of decisions that citizens should make—decisions about the direction institutions should follow and about the actions citizens should take.

Going into a Larger Arena

The examples I've given so far would keep professionals close to their customary roles. This next one is riskier because it would involve educators in matters that some insist aren't any of their business. It would have them enter the larger public arena in ways that would test those restrictions—although educators would not be playing a role inconsistent with the roles they once played in communities (and some still do).

Professional educators might spend more time on community issues that don't have an immediate or direct effect on schools or even, more broadly, education. Some superintendents have already done work along these lines—one by putting town meetings in the schools. The payoff can be a richer understanding of the way citizens go about making up their collective minds on a number of issues. The foundation has called that public thinking.

Certainly teachers and administrators hear from individual citizens every day. But listening to what parents say or what interest groups demand isn't the same as understanding public thinking. Polling data on schools have similar limitations. Concerns about issues other than education influence people's attitudes. Citizens don't just think about schools in isolation; they worry about their medical bills, care for elderly parents, and the landfill proposed for their community.

Simply knowing what troubles citizens or what they want, however, isn't enough. It is impossible to fathom how citizens go about making up their minds when they aren't making up their minds. That's because people think as a public only under certain conditions: they have to be in direct contact with one another and face-to-face with the tensions that are inherent in every major issue.

As discussed in Chapter 6, tensions come about because people hold many things dear, and favoring one often works to the disadvantage of another. Consider the conflicts that citizens have to work through on issues like providing the best possible health care—but at an affordable price. Grappling with what should be done to have the best care—at a price we can afford—makes us stop and think because the price of medical technology is a factor driving up the cost. This is the kind of thinking that professionals in education and school boards need to understand. But the nature of public thinking—the way citizens go about making up their minds—becomes apparent only when educators look at more issues than those that directly affect the schools.

Entering the larger arena of public issues may also be a way of disrupting the cycle of cynicism that entraps all bureaucracies. Brian Cook, mentioned earlier, found that as people become critical of government agencies and press for greater accountability, the agencies responded (or have been required to respond) with measures intended to improve accountability. Yet the remedies have often had just the opposite effect—they have increased the distance between the bureaucracies and citizens, making bureaucracies even less accessible. To break this cycle, Cook calls for the administrators in these bureaucracies to enter into public deliberations on issues that concern citizens, not just the issues that interest bureaucrats.[19] If that is good advice for government administrators, it should be good advice for school administrators.

[19] Brian J. Cook, *Bureaucracy and Self-Government: Reconsidering the Role of Public Administration in American Politics* (Baltimore: Johns Hopkins University Press, 1996), pp. 134-135, 148.

The Kentucky School Boards Association has a project that uses the concept of public thinking and promises to do some of what Cook suggests. The association has sponsored a statewide series of town meetings on issues that affect all the people of Kentucky, such as the social conditions that put young people at risk. As a result, local boards should be in a much better position to understand how the public will approach the issues on board agendas, and they may be able to make their own meetings more deliberative. This project started when school boards recognized that their relationship with the citizens of Kentucky needed to be on more than a "you come help us" basis.[20]

Professionals in other fields have already used deliberative forums to understand the way the public thinks about problems that affect their professions, both directly and indirectly. The American Bar Association (ABA), for instance, has responded to criticism of the judicial system by going directly to the public. The association framed an issue book for forums that presented a range of options for improving the justice system, including some options that probably have little appeal to lawyers.[21]

Meeting criticism, not with counterarguments, but with deliberative reason, as the ABA did, doesn't guarantee that everyone will come to the conclusions the sponsors of forums hope for. Yet the very act of being open to contrary views changes the image of a professional association. Other groups have also put sensitive issues into deliberative formats to engage citizens. For example, the National Advisory Committee on Adult Religious Education (NACARE), a committee of the Department of Education for the U.S. Conference of Catholic Bishops, has used a deliberative guide on abortion in the National Issues Forums series, along with its own supplementary materials. The committee had a broad, public mission—to foster a more informed and responsible citizenry.[22]

---

[20] Kentucky School Boards Association, *Final Report on National Issues Forums and Its Applicability to Local School Boards* (Dayton, OH: Report to the Kettering Foundation, March 22, 2004).

[21] American Bar Association, *"... And Justice for All": Ensuring Public Trust and Confidence in the Justice System* (American Bar Association, 2001).

[22] Tim Grove, ed., *National Issues Forums in the Catholic Community: Handbook for Moderators and Convenors* (National Issues Forums Institute and the United States Conference of Catholic Bishops, 2001), pp. 1, 8, 28.

Perhaps, in time, one of the associations in education will prepare issue books, from the public's perspective, on controversies in education. It might be interesting, for instance, to hear public thinking about the tradeoffs among proposals for improving the quality of teaching.

I don't want to give the impression that encouraging public deliberation is some kind of cure-all for the ills that worry professionals and plague bureaucracies or a way to buff tarnished images. The benefits from engaging citizens in deliberations won't be immediate; the payoff from forums comes only when choice work becomes a habit. And professionals won't know how the public thinks until they have heard from a number of forums—on a variety of issues —held over several years.

Teachers and school administrators entering the larger arena could have one overarching benefit: It might help get professional educators off the defensive in the controversy over the condition of America's public schools. As long as others—politicians, pundits, whoever—are able to tell school folk what the public really thinks, educators are always going to be on the defensive. And efforts to improve our schools are going to be mired in a search for people to blame. Those are reasons enough for educators to engage citizens directly on the major issues of the country.

ON REFLECTION

A reporter once asked me, just after I finished writing another book, what I hoped readers would remember most. In the case of *Reclaiming Public Education*, it would be the questions that drove the research reported in this book—that more than any findings. This book doesn't have definitive answers to any of those questions because they are enduring questions. It does offer ways to think about them that might help people deal with the questions in different and more productive ways. The objective in writing wasn't to overwhelm readers with enough examples and evidence to prove that one answer or another
is right, but rather to make a reasonable case for considering—and perhaps reconsidering—the very nature of the questions we struggle with in education.

The enduring questions have endured so long that they are well known. We are continually asking ourselves what kind of education we want for young people and how much of it should be delegated to schools. Who should be accountable for education? What do we mean when we say our schools are public? And the most basic question of all is, who are we talking about when we talk about the public? This book has taken a different cut at these questions by suggesting other ways of thinking about both the public and education.

The underlying issue in most of these questions is whether the public can be counted on. It is also probably the unspoken question running through the minds of people when they hear arguments for public ownership of the schools. Responding would be difficult enough if the doubts of professional educators were all that had to be put to rest. Chapter 7 recognized that people in positions of authority may have little confidence in the citizens. More worrisome still, studies cited in Chapter 1 showed that citizens themselves have doubts about their fellow citizens, doubts about whether people can count on one another.

Everything said in this book assumes that we must be able to count on the public. Still, doubts persist. In fact, uncertainty about the public has remained pretty much the same since Plato charged that most people have neither the motivation nor intelligence to be responsible citizens. In the 1920s, Walter Lippmann went so far as to argue that the public is a phantom of our political imagination. John Dewey countered Lippmann with the argument that the public is real but unaware of itself or its powers.[1]

The Lippmann-Dewey disagreement has been revived by the latest research on how citizens see their fellow citizens. Having tracked people's views about politics for a decade, Rich Harwood has come to a sobering conclusion: Americans are retreating not only from politics but also from civic life. The country, they have said, is "losing its sense of community." People are a bit ashamed of retreating yet see no alternative. People, desperate to regain some control over their lives, are moving into close-knit circles of family and friends to find a comfort zone. At the same time, they recognize that they should and perhaps could reach out more to others. They are alarmed by what they see as growing social fragmentation and extreme individualism.[2]

The Harwood study and the echoes of the Lippmann-Dewey debate set the stage for the story in this book. And I put them here to press the case that both school folk and citizens in general have a stake in how we deal with threats to democracy, particularly the loss of our sense of community and the erosion of community life. One of the reasons for common public schools was to build a sense of community in a nation of immigrants. Communities of place are also where most schools are located. So the well-being of the school can't be separated from the well-being of the community. If the trends Harwood reports become dominant, both our public schools and our political system will face even more difficulties than they do now.

John Dewey challenged Walter Lippmann's contention that the public was only an illusion, arguing that "the outstanding problem of the Public is discovery and identification of itself." Where are people going to discover themselves as public citizens? Dewey's answer was through the restoration of local community life. Unless that happens,

---

[1] Walter Lippmann, *The Phantom Public* (1927; reprint, New Brunswick, NJ: Transation Publishers, 2004) and John Dewey, *The Public and Its Problems* (Athens, OH: Swallow Press, 1927).

[2] Richard C. Harwood, *Hope Unraveled: The People's Retreat and Our Way Back* (Dayton, OH: Kettering Foundation Press, 2005).

he wrote, "the public cannot adequately resolve its most urgent problem: to find and identify itself."[3] I think Dewey was right. Communities of place are where most people encounter the problems that directly affect their lives. And these communities are where people expect to make a difference in combating those problems.

The only amendment this book makes to Dewey's argument is that the public finds—in fact, creates—itself in community-based public work. Because of the implications for schools and all of education, I believe teachers, administrators, and board members have a special stake in local public building, which is essential in combating the loss of civic self-confidence that Harwood described. All Americans have the same stake; they are right to fear the loss of community. The fact that both school officials and citizens have a stake in combating the same problem illustrates how much the problems of democracy are necessarily the problems of education (just as the reverse is true). More to the point, the role of the public in our political system, which Dewey and Lippmann debated and which concerns citizens today, is the larger version of the question of the role of the public in our educational system—the question of public ownership.

So, can the country count on the public, whether as responsible sovereigns of our democracy or owners of our schools? In the sections on public knowledge and the public thinking that produces it, this book has taken on Plato's criticism that citizens don't have the knowledge to be sovereign. But the Harwood study raises more questions about whether people have the necessary civic self-confidence and sense of community.

Reading between the lines of Harwood's report on *Hope Unraveled*, I see signs of hope enduring. People regret the loss of community, so they must care about it. Harwood's other studies have found that Americans' sense of civic responsibility is not dead. And even in his most recent interviews, people say they should be doing more to join forces with others, which is the primary way citizens have made a difference.

People's doubts about their ability to make a difference are more troubling. If people are as frustrated by their inability to act effectively on their concerns as the Harwood research has shown, they must think they *should* be able to make a difference. That's good news.

---

[3] Dewey, *The Public and Its Problems*, pp. 185, 216.

But they still complain that they lack resources and power. And many individuals are, in fact, without money, legal authority, or the other trappings of conventional power. This book speaks to that doubt in the discussion of other types of power. But one other point needs to be reemphasized.

If we take into account the dynamic qualities of the public and the ability of citizens to form themselves into a public by doing collective work with whatever resources they have at hand, then the public can begin to take shape out of what already exists. It doesn't have to be imported—in fact, it probably can't be because it depends on self-responsibility. The principal resource needed—which community-organizing groups like the Industrial Areas Foundation have discovered—is the ability of people to form pragmatic, working relationships with others in different circumstances and with divergent interests. This is a resource that can't be imported.

The possibility that a democratic public has the equivalents of the self-starters Charles Kettering invented has profound implications for engagement efforts and public building in this country and abroad. So the Kettering Foundation began looking for words to describe an alternative to importing strategies for strengthening democracies. We first hit on "elicitive strategies." "Elicit" seemed on target; it means to "draw forth" something that is perhaps latent or potential. But what a mistake that choice of words proved to be. People twisted their tongues pronouncing "elicitive." The idea, however, was too important to lose. We were convinced that public building could be done by using everyday routines and untapped civic capacities to stimulate public work, rather than bringing citizens to special meetings and introducing them to new information and techniques.

Then we remembered something J. Herman Blake said based on his experience as both a scholar and a community organizer. "Build on what grows," he urged. In nearly every community something is happening to turn conventional routines into public practices or put the public back into the public's business. The key, Blake insisted, is to find what is already trying to happen and build on it. That led him to coin a phrase that reflected the spirit of self-rule. It resonated with the civil rights anthem I cited earlier, "We Are the Ones We Have Been Waiting For."

The best example I have heard of building on what grows came from an American consultant who was asked to advise Russians on improving their industrial productivity. He videotaped exemplary practices in business and showed them to a group of factory managers. They admired what they saw but thought the practices were too advanced to be useful in their plants. The Russians assumed that the best practices came from Western Europe and the United States. Then, the consultant surprised his audience—the videos were all taken in Russian factories! His point was that the plant managers needed to recognize the potential in what was going on around them and build on it.

The alternative to building-on-what-grows politics might be called importing-what-is-missing politics. Importing resources from outside a community may be appropriate in some situations, but this strategy brings a set of problems with it. People have to buy into what is being imported, and new projects have to get up to scale or develop a critical mass. When the importers eventually leave, there has to be an exit plan, which is difficult to put in place without losing the momentum of new projects.

Building on what grows has challenges as well. Perhaps the most formidable is generating respect for local potential and overcoming a culture of low expectations. To repeat: Growing your own resources is not the same as picking yourself up by your bootstraps; all communities have to attract outside resources. Building on what grows also requires producing local goods that can be traded for goods produced outside the community. Harry Boyte explains what this means with examples in his book, *Community Is Possible*, so I won't repeat them here.[4] His favorite, though, is a story of tenants in a housing project trading their collective efforts to paint and landscape for better washers and dryers, which the housing authority provided once officials saw what the tenants were willing to do.

The advantage of building on what grows is that projects can start small and in a number of places. The strategy also assumes that real growth comes in spurts, that two steps forward and one step back is normal. Self-rule can be achieved incrementally, by trial-and-error.

---

[4] Harry C. Boyte, *Community Is Possible: Repairing America's Roots* (New York: Harper and Row, 1984).

I realize that investing in public building seems like going the long way around when educators and board members are confronted by pressing school problems. Community leaders facing a weak economy may react with the same impatience to the suggestion that they create an educational infrastructure in their community before they go out to attract a new industry. Certainly, aligning professional routines with democratic practices is going the long way around when harried school administrators are trying just to get through the day.

In the face of these reservations, public building for public education rests its case on three assumptions: First, public building can create the kind of responsible citizenry that all educational institutions need in order to flourish—a citizenry that is more than a group of consumers. Second, aligning professional routines with democratic practices should not only facilitate public building work but also help overcome some of the friction between educators and citizens. Third, and most important of all, public building protects the foundation of the democracy that gave us our system of public schools. Only a citizenry that rules itself can restore the public schools to their rightful place as democratic institutions still needed to complete the great work of our Revolution.

Bibliography

Alabama General Assembly. *Acts.* 5th biennial sess., 1855-1856. Montgomery: Bates and Lucas, 1856.

Alabama House of Representatives. *Report from the Committee on Education, on the Subject of Public Schools.* Montgomery: Brittan and De Wolf, 1852.

American Bar Association. *"...And Justice for All": Ensuring Public Trust and Confidence in the Justice System.* American Bar Association, 2001.

Annenberg Institute on Public Engagement for Public Education. *Reasons for Hope, Voices for Change.* Providence, RI: Annenberg Institute for School Reform, 1998.

Annual Report of William F. Perry, Superintendent of Education, of the State of Alabama, Made to the Governor, for the Year 1856. Montgomery: Smith and Hughes, 1857.

Barber, Benjamin R. *An Aristocracy of Everyone: The Politics of Education and the Future of America.* New York: Ballantine Books, 1992.

————. *A Place for Us: How to Make Society Civil and Democracy Strong.* New York: Hill and Wang, 1998.

Beauregard, Robert A. "The Public Negotiation of Knowledge." *Higher Education Exchange* (1998): 16-20.

Berry, Wendell. *The Unsettling of America: Culture and Agriculture.* San Francisco: Sierra Club Books, 1986.

Bilby, Sheila Beachum. "Community School Reform: Parents Making a Difference in Education." *Mott Mosaic* 1 (December 2002): 2-7.

Boo, Katherine. "Reform School Confidential: What We Can Learn for Three of America's Boldest School Reforms." *Washington Monthly* 24 (October 1992): 17-24.

Boyte, Harry C. *The Backyard Revolution: Understanding the New Citizen Movement.* Philadelphia: Temple University Press, 1980.

————. "Civic Learning Project: A Project to Strengthen the Civic Dimensions of Teacher Education." (February 2005).

————. *Community Is Possible: Repairing America's Roots.* New York: Harper and Row, 1984.

————. *Everyday Politics: Reconnecting Citizens and Public Life.* Philadelphia: University of Pennsylvania Press, 2004.

Boyte, Harry C., and Nancy N. Kari. *Building America: The Democratic Promise of Public Work.* Philadelphia: Temple University Press, 1996.

Brecher, Jeremy. "'If All the People Are Banded Together': The Naugatuck Valley Project." In *Building Bridges: The Emerging Grassroots Coalition of Labor and Community*, edited by Jeremy Brecher and Tim Costello, 93-105. New York: Monthly Review Press, 1990.

Broder, David S. "Split over Schools . . . Parents and Teachers Disagree on Reforms." *Washington Post*, June 23, 2005.

Bruhn, John G., and Stewart Wolf. *The Roseto Story: An Anatomy of Health.* Norman: University of Oklahoma Press, 1979.

Butler, Nicholas Murray. "Remarks of Dr. Butler, President of Columbia University, before the Merchants' Club, on Saturday, December 8th, at the Auditorium." In *Public Schools and Their Administration: Addresses Delivered at the Fifty-ninth Meeting of the Merchants' Club of Chicago*, 39-51. Chicago: Merchants' Club, 1906.

Christman, Jolley Bruce, and Amy Rhodes. *Civic Engagement and Urban School Improvement: Hard-to-Learn Lessons from Philadelphia.* Consortium for Policy Research Education, June 2002.

Coleman, James S., and Thomas Hoffer. *Public and Private High Schools: The Impact of Communities.* New York: Basic Books, 1987.

Collaborative Communications Group. *New Relationships with Schools: Organizations That Build Community by Connecting with Schools.* Dayton, OH: Report to the Kettering Foundation, May 2003.

Colorado Association of School Boards. *Public Engagement in Five Colorado School Communities.* Dayton, OH: Report to the Kettering Foundation, 2003.

Comer, James P. *Waiting for a Miracle: Why Schools Can't Solve Our Problems—And How We Can.* New York: Dutton, 1997.

Conley, David T. *Roadmap to Restructuring: Policies, Practices, and the Emerging Visions of Schooling.* Eugene: ERIC Clearinghouse on Educational Management, University of Oregon, 1993.

Cook, Brian J. *Bureaucracy and Self-Government: Reconsidering the Role of Public Administration in American Politics.* Baltimore: Johns Hopkins University Press, 1996.

Cremin, Lawrence A. *The American Common School: An Historic Conception.* New York: Bureau of Publications, Teachers College, Columbia University, 1951.

———. *American Education: The Colonial Experience, 1607-1783.* New York: Harper and Row, 1970.

———. *American Education: The Metropolitan Experience, 1876-1980.* New York: Harper and Row, 1988.

———. *American Education: The National Experience, 1783-1876.* New York: Harper and Row, 1980.

———. *Traditions of American Education.* New York: Basic Books, 1977.

———. *The Wonderful World of Ellwood Patterson Cubberly: An Essay on the Historiography of American Education.* New York: Bureau of Publications, Teachers College, Columbia University, 1965.

Crim, Alonzo A. "A Community of Believers Creates a Community of Achievers." *Educational Record* 68/69 (Fall 1987/Winter 1988): 44-49.

Cuban, Larry. "A Solution That Lost Its Problem: Centralized Policymaking and Classroom Gains." In *Who's in Charge Here? The Tangled Web of School Governance and Policy*, edited by Noel Epstein, 104-130. Washington, DC: Brookings Institution Press, 2004.

Davies, Don. "The 10th School Revisited:Are School/Family/Community Partnerships on the Reform Agenda Now?" *Phi Delta Kappan* 83 (January 2002): 388-392.

Dennison, George M. *The Dorr War: Republicanism on Trial, 1831-1861.* Lexington: University of Kentucky Press, 1976.

Derthick, Martha. *Keeping the Compound Republic: Essays on American Federalism.* Washington, DC: Brookings Institution Press, 2001.

Dewey, John. *The Public and Its Problems.* Athens, OH: Swallow Press, 1927.

——. "The School as Social Center." *Elementary School Teacher* 3 (October 1902): 73-86.

Doble Research Associates. *The Comprehensive Educational Resources Inventory: An Analytic Summary of the Results from the CERI Research.* Dayton, OH: Report to the Kettering Foundation, 1994.

——. *A Consumer Mentality: The Prevailing Mind-Set in American Public Education.* Dayton, OH: Report to the Kettering Foundation, 1999.

——. *Education and the Public: Summaries of Five Research Projects.* Dayton, OH: Report to the Kettering Foundation, March 1996.

——. *Expectations and Realities: An Analysis of Existing Research.* Dayton, OH: Report to the Kettering Foundation, January 2004.

——. *How People Connect: The Public and the Public Schools.* Dayton, OH: Report to the Kettering Foundation, June 1998.

——. *Public Schools: Are They Making the Grade?* NIF Report on the Issues. National Issues Forums Institute, 2000.

——. *Reframing "Accountability": The Public's Terms.* Dayton, OH: Report to the Kettering Foundation, March 2001.

——. *Responding to the Critics of Deliberation.* Dayton, OH: Report to the Kettering Foundation, July 1996.

——. *The Story of NIF: The Effects of Deliberation.* Dayton, OH: Kettering Foundation, 1996.

——. *Summaries of Five Research Projects.* Dayton, OH: Report to the Kettering Foundation, April 1995.

——. *Take Charge Workshop Series: Description and Findings from the Field.* Dayton, OH: Report to the Kettering Foundation, 1993.

——. *The Troubled American Family: Which Way Out of the Storm?* NIF Report on the Issues. National Issues Forums Institute, 1996.

————. *Who Is Accountable for Education?* Dayton, OH: Report to the Kettering Foundation, 2003.

Elazar, Daniel J., and John Kincaid. "Covenant and Polity." *New Conversations* 4 (Fall 1979): 4-8.

Evans, Sara M. *Born for Liberty: A History of Women in America.* New York: Free Press, 1989.

Fantini, Mario, Marilyn Gittell, and Richard Magat. *Community Control and the Urban School.* New York: Praeger Publishers, 1970.

Farkas, Steve. *Educational Reform: The Players and the Politics.* Dayton, OH: Public Agenda Report to the Kettering Foundation, 1992.

Farkas, Steve, with Jean Johnson. *Divided Within, Besieged Without: The Politics of Education in Four American School Districts.* New York: Public Agenda Report to the Kettering Foundation, 1993.

Farkas, Steve, and Will Friedman, with Ali Bers. *The Public's Capacity for Deliberation.* Dayton, OH: Public Agenda Report to the Kettering Foundation, 1996.

Fields, Jason. *America's Families and Living Arrangements: 2003.* Washington, DC: U.S. Census Bureau, 2004.

Flynt, Wayne. *Alabama Baptists: Southern Baptists in the Heart of Dixie.* Tuscaloosa: The University of Alabama Press, 1998.

Frank, Glenn. "The Parliament of the People." *Century Magazine* 98 (1919): 401-416.

Fuhrman, Susan, and Marvin Lazerson, eds. *The Public Schools.* Institutions of American Democracy Series. Oxford: Oxford University Press, 2005.

Gallup Organization. *Attitudes toward the Public Schools Survey.* Phi Delta Kappa Survey. May 2003.

Gardner, Howard E. *The Unschooled Mind: How Children Think and How Schools Should Teach.* New York: Basic Books, 1991.

Gastil, John, and Peter Levine, eds. *The Deliberative Democracy Handbook: Strategies for Effective Civic Engagement in the Twenty-first Century.* San Francisco: Jossey-Bass, 2005.

Gelernter, David. "Let's Get Rid of Public Schools." *Virginian-Pilot*, May 22, 2005.

Gillon, Steven M. *"That's Not What We Meant to Do": Reform and Its Unintended Consequences in Twentieth-Century America*. New York: Norton, 2000.

Gittell, Marilyn J. *Limits to Citizen Participation: The Decline of Community Organizations*. Beverly Hills: Sage Publications, 1980.

Gold, Eva, Elaine Simon, and Chris Brown. *Successful Community Organizing for School Reform*. Chicago: Cross City Campaign for Urban School Reform, March 2002.

Goodlad, John I. *A Place Called School: Prospects for the Future*. New York: McGraw-Hill, 2004.

Goodwin, Bryan, and Sheila A. Arens. *No Community Left Behind? An Analysis of the Potential Impact of the No Child Left Behind Act of 2001 on School-Community Relationships*. Dayton, OH: McREL Report to the Kettering Foundation, May 2003.

Gordon, Edmund W., Beatrice L. Bridglall, and Audra Saa Meroe, eds. *Supplementary Education: The Hidden Curriculum of High Academic Achievement*. Lanham, MD: Rowman and Littlefield, 2004.

Grisham, Vaughn L., Jr. *Tupelo: The Evolution of a Community*. Dayton, OH: Kettering Foundation Press, 1999.

Grove, Tim, ed. *National Issues Forums in the Catholic Community: Handbook for Moderators and Convenors*. National Issues Forums Institute and the United States Conference of Catholic Bishops, 2001.

Gutmann, Amy, and Dennis Thompson. *Democracy and Disagreement*. Cambridge, MA: Belknap Press of Harvard University Press, 1996.

Hard Talk: Connecting Education with Our Community. Dayton, OH: Kettering Foundation, 1992.

Hart, Peter D., and Robert M. Teeter. *Equity and Adequacy: Americans Speak on Public School Funding*. Educational Testing Service, June 2004.

Hart, Peter D., and David Winston. *Ready for the Real World? Americans Speak on High School Reform: Executive Summary.* Princeton, NJ: Educational Testing Service, June 2005.

Harvey, Gordon E. *A Question of Justice: New South Governors and Education, 1968-1976.* Tuscaloosa: The University of Alabama Press, 2002.

Harwood, Richard C. *The Engagement Path: The Realities of How People Engage over Time—And the Possibilities for Re-engaging Americans.* Washington, DC: Harwood Institute, October 2003.

———. *Hope Unraveled: The People's Retreat and Our Way Back.* Dayton, OH: Kettering Foundation Press, 2005.

The Harwood Group. *Citizens and Politics: A View from Main Street.* Dayton, OH: Report to the Kettering Foundation, 1991.
———. *Forming Public Capital: Observations from Two Communities.* Dayton, OH: Report to the Kettering Foundation, August 1995.

———. *Halfway out the Door: Citizens Talk about Their Mandate for Public Schools.* Dayton, OH: Report to the Kettering Foundation, 1995.

———. *Hard Talk Discussion Group Report: Insights into How Citizens Talk about Education and Community.* Dayton, OH: Report to the Kettering Foundation, 1991.

———. *How Citizens View Education: Their Public Concerns and Private Actions.* Dayton, OH: Report to the Kettering Foundation, 1993.

———. *Meaningful Chaos: How People Form Relationships with Public Concerns.* Dayton, OH: Kettering Foundation, 1993.

———. *Strategies for Civil Investing: Foundations and Community-Building.* Dayton, OH: Report to the Kettering Foundation, 1997.

The Harwood Institute. *The Public Learning Journey: What It Takes, How to Make It.* Dayton, OH: Report to the Kettering Foundation, 2002.

Heifetz, Ronald A., and Riley M. Sinder. "Political Leadership: Managing the Public's Problem Solving." In *The Power of*

Public Ideas, edited by Robert B. Reich, 179-203. Cambridge, MA: Ballinger Publishing, 1988.

Henderson, Anne T., and Karen L. Mapp. *A New Wave of Evidence: The Impact of School, Family, and Community Connections on School Achievement.* Austin, TX: Southwest Educational Development Laboratory, 2002.

Hill, Paul. "Breaking the Hermetic Seal." *School Administrator Web Edition* (March 2001).

Holladay, J. Mac. *Economic and Community Development: A Southern Exposure.* Dayton, OH: Kettering Foundation, 1992.

Institute for Educational Leadership. *Survey of Parent Involvement.* Washington, DC: Institute for Educational Leadership, 1995.

Isocrates. "Antidosis." In *Isocrates.* Vol. 2, translated by George Norlin, 179-365. 1929. Reprint, New York: G. P. Putnam's Sons, 2000.

Jetter, Alexis. "Mississippi Learning." *New York Times*, February 21, 1993.

Johnson, Gerald. "The Wrong Track: Why Alabamians Believe the State and State's Public Education Are on the Wrong Track." *Alabama School Journal* 121 (June 7, 2004): 1.

Johnson, Jean. "When Experts and the Public Talk Past Each Other." *Connections* (Winter 2005): 27.

Johnson, Jean, et al. *Assignment Incomplete: The Unfinished Business of Education Reform.* New York: Public Agenda, 1995.

Kaestle, Carl F. *Pillars of the Republic: Common Schools and American Society, 1780-1860.* New York: Hill and Wang, 1983.

Kentucky School Boards Association. *Final Report on National Issues Forums and Its Applicability to Local School Boards.* Dayton, OH: Report to the Kettering Foundation, March 22, 2004.

Kotlowski, Dean J. *Nixon's Civil Rights: Politics, Principle, and Policy.* Cambridge, MA: Harvard University Press, 2001.

Kretzmann, John P., and John L. McKnight. *Building Communities from the Inside Out: A Path toward Finding and Mobilizing a Community's Assets.* Evanston, IL: Center for Urban

Affairs and Policy Research, Neighborhood Innovations Network, Northwestern University, 1993.

Lacy, William B. "Democratizing Science in an Era of Expert and Private Knowledge." *Higher Education Exchange* (2001): 52-60.

Lippmann, Walter. *The Phantom Public.* 1927. Reprint, New Brunswick, NJ: Transaction Publishers, 2004.

Lipsky, Michael. *Street-Level Bureaucracy: Dilemmas of the Individual in Public Services.* New York: Russell Sage Foundation, 1980.

Mathews, David. *For Communities to Work.* Dayton, OH: Kettering Foundation, 2002.

————. "Listening to the Public: A New Agenda for Higher Education?" In *Higher Education for the Public Good: Emerging Voices from a National Movement,* edited by Adrianna J. Kezar, Tony C. Chambers, and John C. Burkhardt, 71-86. San Francisco: Jossey-Bass, 2005.

————. *Politics for People: Finding a Responsible Public Voice.* 2d ed. Urbana: University of Illinois Press, 1999.

————. *Why Public Schools? Whose Public Schools? What Early Communities Have to Tell Us.* Montgomery, AL: NewSouth Books, 2003.

Mathews, David, and Noëlle McAfee. *Making Choices Together: The Power of Public Deliberation.* Dayton, OH: Kettering Foundation, 2003.

Mathews, Jay. "Are School Boards Really Necessary?" *Washington Post,* April 10, 2001.

McAndrews, Lawrence J. "Missing the Bus: Gerald Ford and School Desegregation." *Presidential Studies Quarterly* 27 (Fall 1997): 791-804.

McDonald, Nettie S. "I'm Crazy 'Bout Rats." In *Up before Daylight: Life Histories from the Alabama Writers' Project, 1938-1939,* edited by James Seay Brown Jr., 83-85. Tuscaloosa: University of Alabama Press, 1982.

McKnight, John L. "Do No Harm: Policy Options That Meet Human Needs." *Social Policy* 20 (Summer 1989): 5-15.

McWhorter, Diane. *Carry Me Home: Birmingham, Alabama, The Climactic Battle of the Civil Rights Revolution.* New York: Simon and Schuster, 2001.

Meier, Deborah. *In Schools We Trust: Creating Communities of Learning in an Era of Testing and Standardization.* Boston: Beacon Press, 2002.

Mid-continent Research for Education and Learning. *Examining the Meaning of Accountability: Reframing the Construct, A Report on the Perceptions of Accountability.* Dayton, OH: Report to the Kettering Foundation, June 2004.

Morse, Suzanne W. *Smart Communities: How Citizens and Local Leaders Can Use Strategic Thinking to Build a Brighter Future.* San Francisco: Jossey-Bass, 2004.

Mullins, Andrew P., Jr. *Building Consensus: A History of the Passage of the Mississippi Education Reform Act of 1982.* 1992.

Murchland, Bernard. *The Mind of Mamardashvili.* Dayton, OH: An Occasional Paper of the Kettering Foundation, 1991.

Myczack, Leaf. "We're the Solution." *In Context* 28 (Spring 1991): 19.

National School Public Relations Association. *Community Audit.* Dayton, OH: Report to the Kettering Foundation, September 2003.

―――. *NSPRA/Kettering Public Engagement Project: Final Report for July 2002-December 2003.* Dayton, OH: Report to the Kettering Foundation, 2003.

Nielsen, Randall. "Improving Education through Community-Building." *Connections* 11 (February 2001): 9-10.

―――. "Public Schools and the Practices of Engaged Communities." *Connections* (April 2004): 18-21.

Noack, Ernest G. S. "The Satisfaction of Parents with Their Community Schools as a Measure of Effectiveness of the Decentralization of a School System." *Journal of Educational Research* 65 (April 1972): 355-356.

Nye, Joseph S., Jr. "Introduction: The Decline of Confidence in Government." In *Why People Don't Trust Government*, edited by Joseph S. Nye Jr., Philip D. Zelikow, and David C. King, 1-18. Cambridge, MA: Harvard University Press, 1997.

Ohanian, Susan. *Garbage Pizza, Patchwork Quilts, and Math Magic: Stories about Teachers Who Love to Teach and Children Who Love to Learn.* New York: W. H. Freeman, 1992.

Oldenburg, Ray. *The Great Good Place: Cafés, Coffee Shops, Bookstores, Bars, Hair Salons, and Other Hangouts at the Heart of a Community.* New York: Marlowe, 1999.

Olson, Mary, and Naomi Cottoms. *The State of School-Community Relations: Rage and Blame*, Report 2, part 1. *Academic Distress: A Community Issue.* Dayton, OH: Report to the Kettering Foundation, February 2001.

Osborn, Michael, and Suzanne Osborn. *Alliance for a Better Public Voice.* National Issues Forums Institute, 1991.

Owsley, Frank Lawrence. *Plain Folk of the Old South.* 1949. Reprint, with an introduction by Grady McWhiney, Baton Rouge: Louisiana State University Press, 1982.

Paul Werth Associates. *Final Report.* Dayton, OH: Report to the Kettering Foundation, May 5, 2003.

Perdue, Jon. "The Roots of Public Schools." *Kettering Exchange* (Fall 1999): 11-17.

Perry, William F. "The Genesis of Public Education in Alabama." In *Transactions of the Alabama Historical Society: 1897-1898.* Vol. 2, edited by Thomas McAdory Owen, 14-27. Tuscaloosa: Alabama Historical Society, 1898.

———. *Report of the Superintendent of Education of the State of Alabama, to the Governor.* Montgomery: Brittan and Blue, 1855.

Peshkin, Alan. *Growing Up American: Schooling and the Survival of Community.* Chicago: University of Chicago Press, 1978.

Phillips, John Herbert. "Local Taxation for Schools." In *Local Taxation for Schools in Alabama*, 12-20. Montgomery: Phillips-Sheehan, n.d.

Pilisuk, Marc, and Susan Hillier Parks. *The Healing Web: Social Networks and Human Survival.* Hanover, NH: University Press of New England, 1986.

Project Public Life. *The Solomon Project Annual Report.* Minneapolis: Project Public Life, Hubert Humphrey Institute of Public Affairs, 1992.

————. *Teaching Politics: A Report from the Third Annual Project Public Life Working Conference.* Minneapolis: Project Public Life, Humphrey Institute of Public Affairs, 1991.

Public Agenda. *Just Waiting to Be Asked: A Fresh Look at Attitudes on Public Engagement.* New York: Public Agenda, 2001.

————. *On Thin Ice: How Advocates and Opponents Could Misread the Public's Views on Vouchers and Charter Schools.* New York: Public Agenda, 1999.

————. *Playing Their Parts: Parents and Teachers Talk about Parental Involvement in Public Schools.* New York: Public Agenda, 1999.

————. *Teaching Interrupted: Do Discipline Policies in Today's Public Schools Foster the Common Good?* New York: Public Agenda for Common Good, May 2004.

Public Agenda Foundation with the Center for Foreign Policy Development at Brown University. *The Superpowers: Nuclear Weapons and National Security.* National Issues Forums, Domestic Policy Association, 1987.

Public Education Network. *All for All: Strengthening Community Involvement for All Students.* Washington, DC: Public Education Network, 2000.

Public Education Network and *Education Week. Learn. Vote. Act.: The Public's Responsibility for Public Education.* 2004.

Puriefoy, Wendy. "All for All: Citizens Say They Want to Support the Public Schools." *American School Board Journal* (April 2000): 36-38.

Putnam, Robert D. *Bowling Alone: The Collapse and Revival of American Community*. New York: Simon and Schuster, 2000.

———. "Community-Based Social Capital and Educational Performance." In *Making Good Citizens: Education and Civil Society*, edited by Diane Ravitch and Joseph P. Viteritti, 58-95. New Haven: Yale University Press, 2001.

———. *Making Democracy Work: Civic Traditions in Modern Italy*. Princeton, NJ: Princeton University Press, 1993.

Putnam, Robert D., and Lewis M. Feldstein. *Better Together: Restoring the American Community*. New York: Simon and Schuster, 2003.

Quist, John W. *Restless Visionaries: The Social Roots of Antebellum Reform in Alabama and Michigan*. Baton Rouge: Louisiana State University Press, 1998.

Report of Gabriel B. DuVal, Superintendent of Education, of the State of Alabama, Made to the Governor, for the Year 1858. Montgomery: Shorter and Reid, 1859.

Report of William F. Perry, Superintendent of Education, of the State of Alabama, Made to the Governor, for the Year 1857. Montgomery: N. B. Cloud, 1858.

Resnick, Lauren B. "Learning In School and Out." *Educational Researcher* 16 (December 1987): 13-20.

Rittel, Horst W. J., and Melvin M. Webber. "Dilemmas in a General Theory of Planning." *Policy Sciences* 4 (1973): 155-169.

Robertson, David Brian, ed. *Loss of Confidence: Politics and Policy in the 1970s*. University Park: Pennsylvania State University Press, 1998.

Rokeach, Milton, and Sandra J. Ball-Rokeach. "Stability and Change in American Value Priorities, 1968-1981." *American Psychologist* 44 (May 1989): 775-784.

Rose, Lowell C., and Alec M. Gallup. "The 37th Annual Phi Delta Kappa/Gallup Poll of the Public's Attitudes toward the Public Schools." *Phi Delta Kappan* 87 (September 2005): 41-57.

Rothstein, Richard. *Class and Schools: Using Social, Economic, and Educational Reform to Close the Black-White Achievement Gap.* Washington, DC: Economic Policy Institute, 2004.

Sanders, Mavis G., Joyce L. Epstein, and Lori Connors-Tadros. *Family Partnerships with High Schools: The Parents' Perspective.* Center for Research on the Education of Students Placed at Risk, February 1999.

Schön, Donald A. *Educating the Reflective Practitioner: Toward a New Design for Teaching and Learning in the Professions.* San Francisco: Jossey-Bass, 1987.

————. *The Reflective Practitioner: How Professionals Think in Action.* New York: Basic Books, 1983.

Schulman, Bruce J. *The Seventies: The Great Shift in American Culture, Society, and Politics.* New York: Free Press, 2001.

Seebach, Linda. "Government Runs Schools No Better Than It Would Churches." *Dayton Daily News*, January 19, 1995.

Sexton, Robert F. *Mobilizing Citizens for Better Schools.* New York: Teachers College Press, 2004.

Shelton, Jack. *Consequential Learning: A Public Approach to Better Schools.* Montgomery, AL: NewSouth Books, 2005.

Skocpol, Theda. *Diminished Democracy: From Membership to Management in American Civic Life.* Norman: University of Oklahoma Press, 2003.

Sokoloff, Harris. "A Deliberative Model for Engaging the Community: Use of Community Forums Can Undercut Special-Interest Politics." *School Administrator* 53 (November 1996): 12-18.

Stecher, Brian, and Sheila Nataraj Kirby, eds. *Organizational Improvement and Accountability: Lessons for Education from Other Sectors.* Santa Monica, CA: RAND Corporation for the William and Flora Hewlett Foundation, 2004.

Stone, Clarence N. "The Dilemmas of Social Reform Revisited: Putting Civic Engagement in the Picture." Paper presented at the annual meeting of the American Political Science Association, Atlanta, GA, September 2-5, 1999.

————. "Linking Civic Capacity and Human Capital Formation." In *Strategies for School Equity: Creating Productive Schools in a Just Society*, edited by Marilyn J. Gittell, 163-176. New Haven: Yale University Press, 1998.

Sullivan, William. *Work and Integrity: The Crisis and Promise of Professionalism in America.* New York: HarperBusiness, 1995.

Sumners, Joe A., with Christa Slaton and Jeremy Arthur. *Building Community: The Uniontown Story.* Dayton, OH: Report to the Kettering Foundation, 2005.

Thomas, Jennie Vanetta Carter. "How Three Governors Involved the Public in Passing Their Education Reform Programs." EdD diss., George Peabody College for Teachers of Vanderbilt University, 1992.

Traub, James. "What No School Can Do." *New York Times Magazine* (January 16, 2000): 52.

Tyack, David, and Larry Cuban. *Tinkering toward Utopia: A Century of Public School Reform.* Cambridge, MA: Harvard University Press, 1995.

Tyack, David, and Elizabeth Hansot. *Managers of Virtue: Public School Leadership in America, 1820-1980.* New York: Basic Books, 1982.

Umphrey, Michael L. "Tinkling Cymbals and Sounding Brass: Hearing the Different Drum." Featured author presentation, Montana Education Association/Montana Federation of Teachers Annual Conference, Billings, MT, October 16, 2003.

UNM Institute for Public Policy. *A Builder's Guide to Public Deliberation: An Executive Summary of "Understanding Public Deliberation."* Dayton, OH: Report to the Kettering Foundation, 1995.

U.S. Department of Education. National Center for Education Statistics. "1.1 Million Homeschooled Students in the United States in 2003." *Issue Brief* (July 2004).

Warren, Mark R. *Dry Bones Rattling: Community Building to Revitalize American Democracy.* Princeton, NJ: Princeton University Press, 2001.

Welter, Rush. *Popular Education and Democratic Thought in America.* New York: Columbia University Press, 1962.

West Virginia Center for Civic Life. *Ties That Bind: West Virginians Talk about Their Relationship with Public Schools.* Charleston: West Virginia Center for Civic Life, October 2000.

What Citizens Can Do: A Public Way to Act. Dayton, OH: Kettering Foundation, 1999.

Wiebe, Robert H. *Self-Rule: A Cultural History of American Democracy.* Chicago: University of Chicago Press, 1995.

Yankelovich, Daniel. *Coming to Public Judgment: Making Democracy Work in a Complex World.* Syracuse: Syracuse University Press, 1991.

―――――. *New Rules: Searching for Self-Fulfillment in a World Turned Upside Down.* New York: Random House, 1981.

INDEX

Civic activities, 96

Civic capacity, 57, 62, 114

Civic commitment, 83, 100-101

Civic learning, 84, 103-105

Civic life, 138

Civic responsibility, 12, 114
    See also Responsibility

Clinton, Gov. Bill, 39

Collaboration, xii, 62-67, 119, 121, 129-130

Collective action, vii, 44-46, 88

Collective decision making, xi, 117-119
    choice work, 94, 96, 109-113
    deliberation, 92-94
    framing, 88
    after learning, 104
    naming, 88
    and self-rule, vii
    See also Deliberation

Collective learning, 84, 103-105

Collective responsibility, xiii, 4
    See also Responsibility

Colorado Association of School Boards, 123

Community, xiii, 5, 13, 14, 45, 46, 51, 110, 138
    accountability, 13, 14, 15-17
    alienation of, 29
    analyzing problems, 125-126
    assessment, 84, 103-105
    attitudes, 33-34, 115
    auditing, 124-126
    and democratic practices, 85-106
    and education, 3, 57
    as educator, 57-59, 60, 62, 66, 129
    leaderful, 115-116, 119
    and reforms, 35-39

resources, 112, 141
    and schools, 5, 6, 12, 18, 22
    sense of, 5, 138
    smart, 97
    See also Citizens; Public

Community building, xiv, 23,104
    See also Public building

Community Is Possible, 141

Community organizations, 121-122

Confidence, 7, 112-113

Consumers, 43-44, 45, 46
    and bureaucracy, 51

Cook, Brian, 50-51, 134-135

Cremin, Lawrence, 127

D

Dayton, OH, 128

Decision making. *See* Collective decision making

Deliberation, 83, 92-99, 100, 105, 109-113, 135
    after learning, 104
    opportunities for, 117-119
    See also Collective decision making; Forums

Democracy, viii, 142
    and communities, xiii
    and deliberation, 94-99
    and educated citizenry, viii
    and engagement, 77-82
    and institutions, 8
    problems of, 13
    and public education, v, vi
    and schools, 18, 67
    and self-rule, vii
    and values, viii, 85-88

Democratic practices, 85-106, 109, 113, 122-123, 130-133
    auditing, 124-126